Glass Architecture by Paul Scheerbart

Alpine Architecture by Bruno Taut

Portrait of Paul Scheerbart by Oskar Kokoschka. Published in Der Sturm, *no. 15/16, 1915.*

Glass Architecture

by Paul Scheerbart

and

Alpine Architecture

by Bruno Taut

Edited with an introduction by Dennis Sharp

Glass Architecture translated
by James Palmes

Alpine Architecture translated
by Shirley Palmer

Praeger Publishers
New York · Washington

BOOKS THAT MATTER

Published in the United States of America in 1972
by Praeger Publishers, Inc.,
111 Fourth Avenue, New York, N.Y. 10003.

Library of Congress Catalog Card Number: 70-183059

Printed in Great Britain

Produced by November Books Limited.
Designed by Tom Carter and John Leath.
House Editor: Celia Phillips

Contents

Paul Sheerbart's Glass World

An introductory essay by

Dennis Sharp

In this book the prophetic poet and the visionary architect share a common dream of a world revivified by glass architecture. For the first time two texts are brought together in an English translation which both – in quite separate ways – indicate the validity of the argument for an architecture of glass and steel which was put forward over fifty years ago. The theorist of this glass architecture was the Berlin Bohemian poet and novelist Paul Scheerbart (1863–1915); the designer who put the skin and bones on the concept was Bruno Taut, uncrowned leader of the circle of revolutionary architects which emerged in Berlin after World War I. Paul Scheerbart's book *Glasarchitektur*, published in 1914 in Berlin, provided a programmatic outline for the new glass architecture: Bruno Taut's *Alpine Architektur*,[1] published in 1919 at Hagen by the Folkwang Press, was one attempt to express the programme in visual terms. There were others, including Taut's *Die Auflösung der Städte* (1920), which was an elaboration of the schemes in *Alpine Architektur*, and sub-titled *Der Weg zur Alpine Architektur*, the first part of which was to become a catchword of modern architecture.[2]

Glasarchitektur has been considered by generations of architectural critics and historians to be a document of paramount importance, and many, from Adolf Behne to Reyner Banham, have emphasised its germinative role in the development of 20th-century architecture. Behne referred to the book as 'the foundation of modern architecture' soon after it was published in 1914 and Banham – who was instrumental in bringing Scheerbart to the notice of English readers with his article 'The Glass Paradise' in 1959[3] – has more recently written that 'of all the visionary writings of that period, this book has the greatest impact nowadays as the concrete and tangible vision of the future environment of man'.[4]

That it should have remained untranslated until now is not simply an accident of history, but is partly due to the rarity of the original limited edition and to the antagonism that has existed until quite recently to 'things German'. By ignoring *Glasarchitektur*, or by simply being unaware of its existence or its place in the sources of the modern movement, successive generations of English-speaking historians have overlooked a primary tract prophetic of much about modern architecture that is commonplace today, from the glass and concrete boxes of city centres to the idea of transportable buildings. If the book is known at all widely then this has been through the odd bits (often taken out of context) that have appeared in architectural surveys and anthologies. The actual pithy, witty and provocative text has now been rescued from the past and the myths surrounding the phrase 'glass architecture' can be dispelled; as Behne wrote in 1918, it 'is not the crazy caprice of a poet that glass architecture will bring a new culture. *It is a fact!*' Who would now dispute that he was right?

But the credit should not all go to Scheerbart. Many of the hundreds of books – in German and English – that were produced on horticultural and exhibition buildings in the 19th century had indicated the validity of an architecture in glass and iron, not only for botanical purposes but also for human concourse and habitation. Paxton in 1851 had even shown that this could be done on a vast scale with his Crystal Palace, while John Ruskin had been exhorting members of the Architectural Association in 1857 to contemplate, of all things, a glass dome over London. He said:

If your style be of the ideal kind, you shall wreath your streets with ductile

Bruno Taut (1880–1938).

leafage, and roof them with variegated crystal – you shall put, if you will, all London *under one blazing dome of many colours* [my italicising] that shall light the clouds round it with its flashing as far as the sea. And still, I ask you, What after this? Do you suppose those imaginations of yours will ever lie down there asleep beneath the shade of your iron leafage, or within the coloured light of your enchanted dome?

Architectural historians have often been accused of searching out obscure

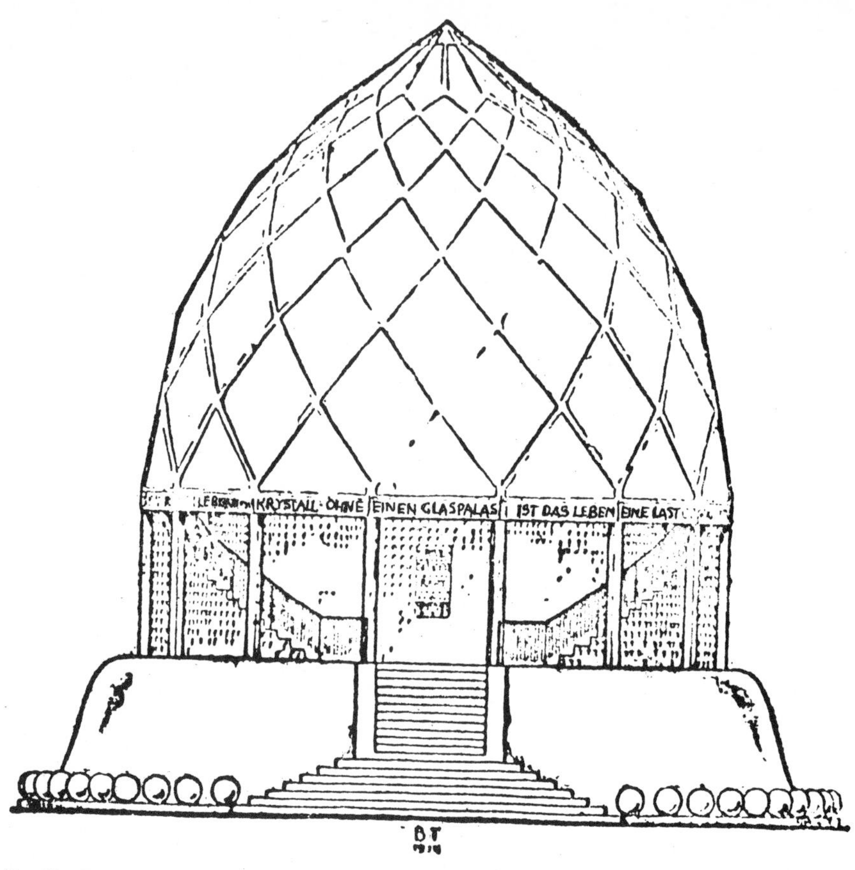

DER GOTISCHE DOM IST DAS PRALUDIUM DER GLASARCHITEKTUR

Right: The Glass Pavilion, Werkbund Exhibition, Cologne, 1914. The Glass House was approached only from one side and to balance the entrance Taut placed the mechanical equipment required for the pavilion in a bulge in the substructure on the other side. The decorative balls around the base were also of glass. Above: Bruno Taut's drawing for the Glass Pavilion, from the opening programme of the exhibition.

correspondences in literature to support statements about 'influences' on the work of particular architects. In the case of the connection between Scheerbart and Taut there can be no dissension, as enough evidence exists to prove a correspondence of ideas as well as a mutual admiration and personal friendship. Their first contact goes back to the early days of Herwarth Walden's magazine *Der Sturm*, and by the end of 1913, when Paul Scheerbart's *Glasarchitektur* was in manuscript, he and Taut were in regular correspondence. In May 1914 Bruno Taut, together with his brother Max and their partner Franz Hoffman

(who was site architect for the project), erected a small domed glass pavilion at Cologne for the German Werkbund Exhibition of that year. Scheerbart's book (which appeared under the *Sturm* imprint just before the older poet had opened the pavilion), and the 'Glass house' itself were mutually dedicated. Like so many exhibition buildings before and since it was a premonition of what architecture might become as well as an advertisement for its sponsors – the German glass industries – on the way new materials might be exploited. It crystallised the Scheerbartian concept of an architecture of glass and concrete. The size of the pavilion belittled its importance as one of the most technologically advanced experimental structures at the Cologne show and although it was missed off the official Werkbund layout plan of the exhibition it has since found its place alongside the other two pioneering buildings at Cologne: Walter Gropius's Model Factory and Henri van de Velde's Model Theatre.

Even so it was not exactly a brilliant piece of architecture (few experimental buildings ever are), and one cannot help contemplating what the building would have been like if Scheerbart had been the designer and not Taut! In fact neither Scheerbart nor Taut were trained architects.

The planning of the Glass house was a typical piece of Prussian monumentalism with a solid concrete podium and a central axis – as classically organised as Bramante's Tempietto in S. Pietro in Montorio at Rome, and perhaps, relatively speaking, a direct descendant, although both Scheerbart and Taut claimed that the Gothic was the 'prelude' to their glass architecture ideas.

The technical advances are to be seen in the use of glass and in the construction of the double glazed prismatic dome which surmounted a 14-sided concrete and glass drum. This polyhedric cupola was constructed from small section concrete ribs and the resulting rhomboid spaces were glazed on the outside in clear plate glass and on the inside with 'Luxfer' prisms backed with sheets of coloured glass. The total effect was by all accounts startling both from the outside, which shone at night like a jewel, and from the inside where the effect was heightened by the play of coloured light from a mechanical kaleidoscope. In a sense Taut's Glass house was an early prototype of the multi-media – or psychedelic – pavilions that are now commonly found at international exhibitions. In addition to the play with light the designer also introduced a continuously flowing cascade of water at the base of the pavilion, as well as an aural background of piped music.

Interior of the lower floor of the Glass House showing the water basin and the glass mosaics and cartoons.

Glass was everywhere; walls, ceilings, floors, and even staircases were all finished in some kind of translucent or transparent material. Taut's aim was 'the enclosure of space by means of glass' and he playfully introduced coloured glass, opaque glass and clear glass to create various effects of distance, silhouette and nearness. The main space of the exhibition pavilion rose through two floors and the lower part, in which the water basin was situated, contained a number of glass mosaics and cartoons let into the glass wall surfaces. These designs emphasised the difference between the opaque and coloured surfaces and showed how a picture could be fitted into a seemingly limitless frame. Taut was far more interested in these types of experiment than was the '*es ist da, und es ist nicht da*' glass philosophy of later Berlin functionalist architects such as Arthur Korn. Glass in 1914 was being tested by Taut as a vehicle for expression rather than as an adjunct to a philosophy of a 'new' or 'modern' architecture of the type envisaged in Germany after 1924. It was essentially a propagandist move.

To reinforce the message of glass architecture and the future it afforded,

Bruno Taut invited Scheerbart to provide *bon mots* to go round the 14 sides of the pavilion. Scheerbart wrote a letter to Taut in February 1914 complaining that he had struggled for some time with 14 mottoes of 28 words before he realised that his request had been for mottoes with a maximum of 28 letters each. A number of the mottoes were eventually used and incised into the concrete beam at the base of the dome. The phrases themselves were clever rhyming couplets which do not translate well into English. However, even in the rhythm (for instance, *Glück ohne Glas – Wie dumm ist das!*) has gone, the original meaning is still there; these are the 14 phrases that Scheerbart sent to Taut:

1 Happiness without glass
How crass!

2 Bricks may crumble
Coloured glass endures

3 Coloured glass
Destroys hatred

4 Coloured happiness
Only comes in a glass culture

5 Without a glass palace
Life becomes a burden

6 A glass house does not catch fire
There is no need for a fire brigade [5]

7 Parasites are not nice
They will never get into the glass house

8 Combustible materials
Are a scandal

9 Greater than the diamond
Is the double walled glass house

10 Light permeated the Universe
It comes to life in the crystal

11 The prism is marvellous
That is why the glass house is great!

12 By shunning colour
One sees nothing of the Universe

13 Glass makes everything light
So use it on the site

14 Glass opens up a new age
Brick building only does harm.

After the war, Taut was immediately able to publish the work that had absorbed him during the fallow war years and indicate in his pronouncements for the active revolutionary groups in Berlin that the glass architecture ideas were still current. 'Paul Scheerbart, our protective spirit, will have to guide us', he wrote about his dead hero; 'Paul Scheerbart will remove the bandage from your eyes and at last you will see . . . Architects, here is your world, enter this brilliant poet's world and smile.' The two groups with which Taut most closely associated himself, the *Arbeitsrat für Kunst* and the less specific and more personal group of corresponding associates which became known as *Die gläserne Kette*, followed his injunction. The Scheerbartian ideas were disseminated throughout these groups.

The second book publication of the *Arbeitsrat*, *Ruf zum Bauen* (Call to Building) was dedicated to 'the spirit of Paul Scheerbart' and almost all the corresponding members of Taut's Glass Chain became absorbed in preparing glass architecture projects.[6]

But what do we know of this extraordinary personality, Paul Scheerbart? Very little I am afraid. Taut was well aware of his importance as a literary figure and wrote in 1919, 'To those that do not know his name let it be said, that in 50 years time he will rank among the German classical writers.' Well, not quite true yet, but I have no doubt that this prediction will eventually be proved correct and Scheerbart will obtain his rightful place in books on literature, along with

Right: Title page of Glasarchitektur *published by Verlag der Sturm in 1914.*

Glasarchitektur

von

Paul Scheerbart

Verlag der Sturm / Berlin W 9

1914

Wedekind and all the others. At the moment he is considered a figure of minor importance. Scheerbart is represented in most standard German literary histories of the 20th century and an anthology of his writings appeared to coincide with the fiftieth anniversary of his death, but so far no critical publications exist that shed any new light on his life and views. It is therefore far from easy to give a clear picture of Scheerbart's background, as he still merges into the shadows of the history of both literature and architecture.

He was born in Danzig on 8 January 1863, the eleventh child of a father who died four years after his birth. His mother also died when he was young and he was brought up by relatives. In his early youth he studied theology, but soon developed an interest in contemporary philosophy. At the age of 30, when he had become known in Berlin as a poet and freelance writer, he founded his own underground press, *Verlag Deutsche Phantasten*, and published his first book, *Das Paradies, die Heimat der Kunst*. By the mid-nineties he was associating with the various intellectual and literary circles in Berlin. Rudolf Steiner in his memoirs records meeting him a number of times. He was, Steiner wrote 'an entirely lovable' man, but entirely unfathomable, an eccentric whom Steiner places alongside Frank Wedekind as one of the 'personalities' of *fin de siècle* Berlin who brought an 'unlimited enrichment' to life. Steiner portrays him as a man of singularly unprepossessing appearance, looking in the nineties like a 'bureaucrat, somewhat lifted up into the spiritual . . . quite ordinary, commonplace' – entirely different from the later impression given by the famous Kokoschka portrait of about 1910 which indicates a gross, seedy, avuncular figure. But by the time Kokoschka had drawn his portrait, and indeed by the time Taut had got to know him well, Scheerbart and his wife, neither of whom had any interest in material possessions, had descended into abject poverty and were living without even a table or chairs, largely forgotten by the older generation but revered by the young – 'the finest mind in Europe', one of the Expressionists wrote in 1912. After a period of ill health Scheerbart died on 15 October 1915.

Two decades earlier he had been in the midst of Bohemian life. Steiner remembered him as a key figure in Hartleben's Berlin circle, producing poems which possessed at first reading seemingly 'arbitrary' combinations of words, that on closer examination revealed 'unobserved meanings' which strove 'to bring to expression a spiritual content derived from a fantasy of soul'. Steiner goes on: 'In Paul Scheerbart there was a vital inner cult of the fantastic, but one that moved in the . . . forms of the grotesque.'

Scheerbart was absorbed in lexicological problems, wit, and the element that Steiner refers to as the 'grotesque' – qualities which emerge in *Glasarchitektur*, and in the few drawings he made to illustrate his own books. His drawings are of a very different order to those of Taut and include (in available published sources at least), depictions of hairy bizarre creatures – half human, half animal – from a very peculiarly cerebral zoo all dotted out in ink in a *pointilliste* technique, as well as swirling *Jugendstil* ornamental borders. Scheerbart anticipated the current French obsession with *La Fantastique*, that semi-surrealist erotic madness to be seen today in the work of artists like Hans Bellmar and Bertrand. He was not, however, an eroticist and only one of his books, *Tarub, Bagdads berühmte Köchin*, 1900, employs this theme. Most of his books are critical

Drawings by Paul Scheerbart from volumes 1, 2 and 3 of his six-volume Revolutionären Theater-Bibliothek, *1904*.

A drawing by Scheerbart from Den Dokumenten des Fortschritts, *no. 2., 1908.*

Right: A series of self portraits by Scheerbart from the Hippopotamus novel Immer Mutig, *1902.*

commentaries on prevailing trends of the times in which he either condemns the current philistinism or extrapolates future worlds. His writings on architecture, which began as early as 1900, are slanted to what we would now call 'Futuristics'.

During the heyday of Bohemian Berlin in the 1890s, those halcyon days of self-indulgence, individualism and jollity, Scheerbart was an important member of the decadent circle of Satanists centred on Stanislaus Pryzbyszewski, and met through his associates such visiting demons as Auguste Strindberg. He was sufficiently well known at the time to be satirised by the popular author Otto Julius Bierbaum as '*der Barenführer*' in his novel of 1897, *Stilpe: Roman aus der Froschperspectiv*. From that time a flood of publications by Scheerbart followed right up until his death, many bearing such seemingly improbable descriptions

RAKKÓX DER BILLIONAER / EIN PROTZENROMAN ⁂ DIE WILDE JAGD / EIN ENTWICKLUNGSROMAN IN ACHT ANDEREN GESCHICHTEN VON PAUL SCHEERBART / MIT BUCHSCHMUCK VON JOSSOT UND EINER ILLUSTRATION VON FELIX VALLOTTON ⁂ IM INSEL-VERLAG G. m. b. H. LEIPZIG ⁂ WEIHNACHTEN MDCCCCI ⁂

of their contents as a 'railway novel with 66 intermezzos', an 'Arabian Culture novel', 'a fantastic hippopotamus novel', and others on a space fiction theme, such as 'Astral pantomime' and 'Moon novel'. It was in the 'snobbish' novel

of 1900, *Rakkox, der Billionär*, that Scheerbart introduced his first architectural theme and sought for a future world transformed by architecture. In *The Emperor of Utopia*, a 'folk' novel of 1904, he attacked conventional art and

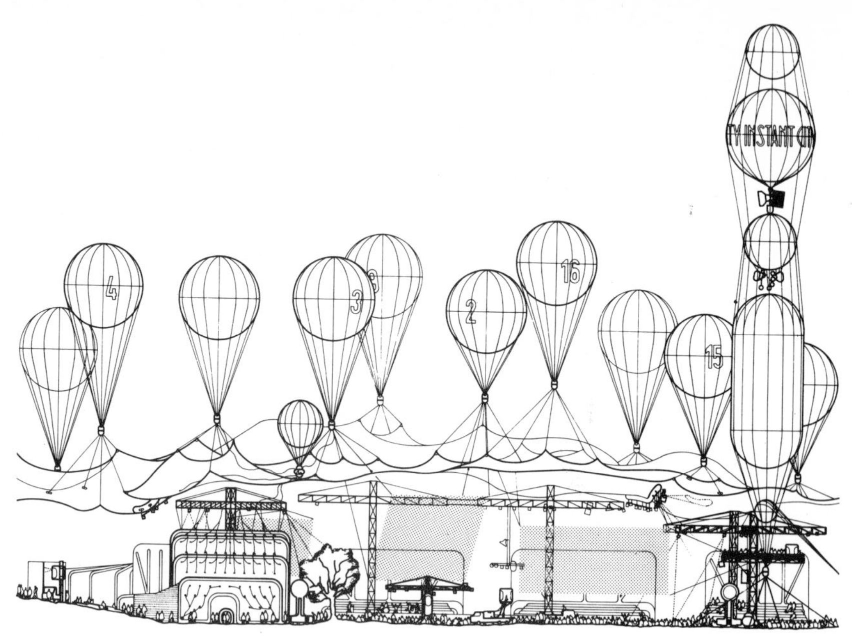

Peter Cook, Instant City, 1969.

philistinism and depicted the rise of an avant-garde counter movement (perhaps a premonition of the post war *Arbeitsrat für Kunst* in which Taut was to play an important role), that consisted of 'painters, sculptors, and especially architects', who were 'possessed by a keen desire to live in the future'. The futurological emphasis was surprisingly prophetic. In this Utopian novel Scheerbart put forward his ideas for transportable houses and transportable cities which were, in his view, to be the particular distinguishing features of the future. But even for such a futurist there was a practical side to his proposals (as there was in his later glass architecture ideas), and in the Emperor's Utopia a note of remarkable economic restraint occurs. He wrote:

> Naturally such costly plans for the future could not be immediately translated into reality. Therefore it was decided to arrange first an artist's fair with small transportable restaurants. Twenty very large captive balloons were supposed to lift the restaurants into the air, there to ascend and descend in interesting combinations, thus displaying the charms of a mobile architecture.

It was left to future generations to put skin and bones on that notion; it recurs a number of times in the late 1920s and early 1930s (Leonidov's projects in the USSR), and most recently in Peter Cook's Instant City project of 1969.

In 1908 Scheerbart wrote a short article in a German arts magazine, *Morgen*, proposing – surely for the first time – an automobile theatre. *Glasarchitektur*

Left: Osram Publicity Tower, Berlin, 1929.

Right: The Philips Company Light Column, Amsterdam, 1929.

itself abounds with inventions and predictions for glass, many of which we now take for granted, from double glazing, heat sources in cavities of glass, electrically heated carpets, self-opening doors (which he notes had already been patented in Berlin), air conditioning and movable glass partitions, to the large-scale ideas of 'night architecture', and glass towers in cities: 'Towns and other places should always be distinguished by towers. Every effort must naturally be made to lend enchantment to towers by night. Under the rule of glass architecture, therefore, all towers must become towers of light.' There are others, but it would spoil the continuity of Scheerbart's text if I disclose too many of his rich thoughts here.

It was only a few years before many of these innovations and ideas became a reality, at first on paper during that extraordinarily fertile period of Utopian dreaming in Berlin immediately after World War I, and later through the buildings of the modern 'functionalist' architects themselves. The paper visionaries, like the pioneer architects of the earlier decade and the later functionalists, were unanimous in their admiration for the achievements of the great 19th-century engineers and their glass and iron technology. Paul Scheerbart and Bruno Taut had provided the transition which made glass architecture a viable æsthetic concept. 'The *Glashaus* has no other purpose than to be beautiful', wrote Bruno Taut in a pamphlet produced for the opening of his pavilion in 1914 – 'Glass architecture is also a compelling influence on applied art and art in general', Scheerbart had written the year before.

The correspondents of the Glass Chain were nearly all (with the exceptions of Walter Gropius and the biomorphic individualist Hermann Finsterlin), absorbed

Utopian sketch by Hans Scharoun, 1920.

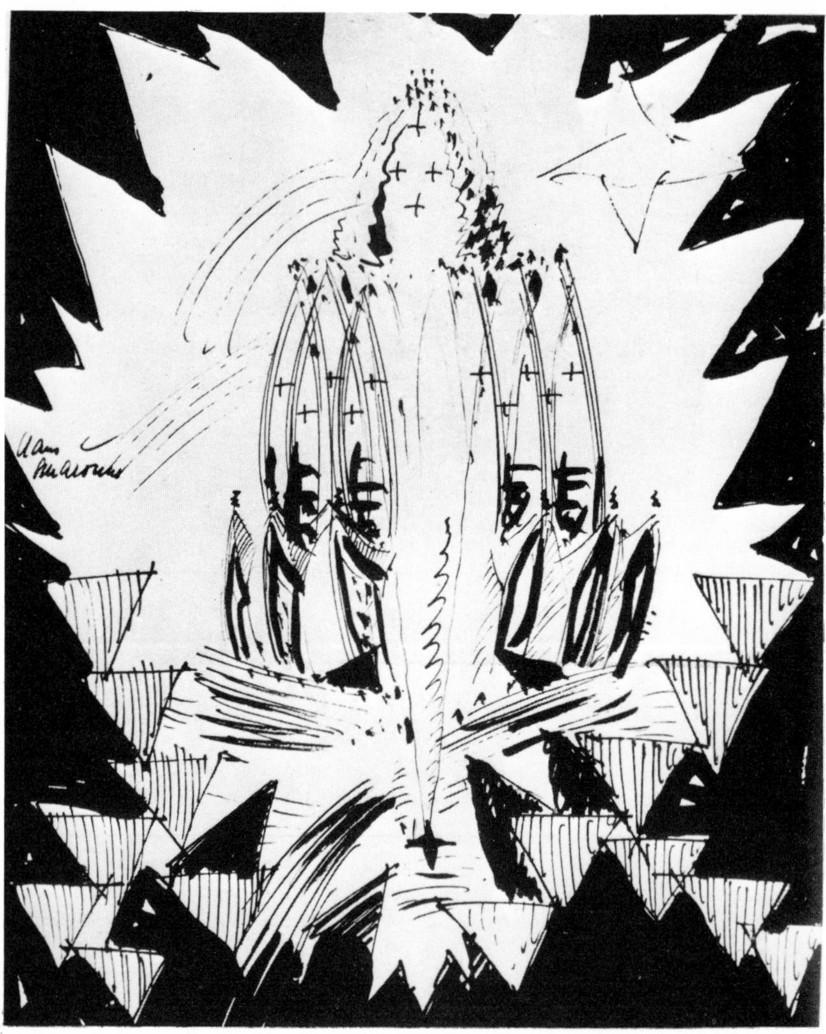

with questions of the æsthetics of the new glass architecture, as the title of the group suggests. The numerous projects produced during the period of 'paper architecture' (from 1919–21) explore the formal problem of designing in glass: from Hans Scharoun, the mascot of the group, the exciting combination of glass

Mies van der Rohe, model of glass skyscraper, 1920–1.

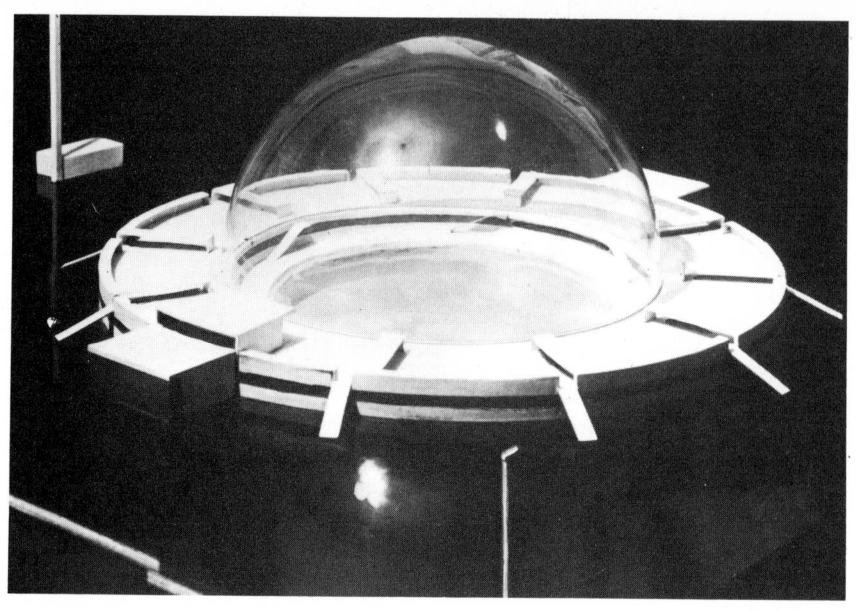

L. Nikolski, swimming bath project, USSR, 1927.

and coloured light produced explosive graphic descriptions on the recurring theme of 'palaces for the people'; for the Luckhardt brothers – who were far more critical of Taut's views than others in the group – it brought to the surface a desire to depict the transcendental and colourful world of the Gothic in the form of modern 'cultural centres', while for Wenzel Hablik a crystal geometry emerged in a philosophy he called '*Cyklus Architektur*', based on the manipulation of faceted surfaces of domes and towers of indefinite height.

Outside Taut's group, others were exploring similar ground. Mies van der Rohe designed his most uncharacteristic glass skyscrapers in 1921–2 with their freely curved surfaces determined by three major factors (all intuitive, it must be said): 'sufficient illumination of the interior, the massing of the building viewed from the street, and lastly the play of reflections'. In 1925 Peter Behrens built his glass pavilion for the Paris Exhibition of that year and this building, together with the house for Dr Dalsace in Paris by Bijvoet and Duiker in 1929–31, perhaps best of all shows the validity of Scheerbart's thesis.

By the end of the decade the glass dream had come true and two publications were produced primarily to feature through selected examples the advantages to be gained by designing in glass. K. Werner Schulze's *Glas in der Architektur der Gegenwart* and Arthur Korn's *Glas im Bau und als Gebrauchsgegenstand*[7] provided a catalogue of master examples of glass architecture: Schulze's book opens with a lengthy dissertation on Scheerbart's ideas and was dedicated to his spirit.

Bruno Taut by this time was out of the running. From 1919–22 he had edited his magazine *Frühlicht* and had used it, among other things, as a vehicle for promoting glass architecture and for publishing his correspondence with his friends. The last year of publication was from Magdeburg where he had moved in 1921 and become *Stadtbaurat* (City Engineer). A year or so later he was back in Berlin, and a partner again in the practice of his brother Max. Having moved into the realm of practical building, having warned his generation about the dissolution of the city and offered them his vision of a new environment, his own work reverted to the dull brick and window tradition he had so much abhorred. For Taut the spark had gone out.

Surprisingly it was Frank Lloyd Wright who took up, probably without knowledge of *Glasarchitektur*, the Scheerbartian views. He wrote in the *Architectural Record* in July 1928:

Imagine a city iridescent by day, luminous by night, imperishable! Buildings, shimmering fabrics, woven of rich glass; glass all clear or part opaque and part clear, patterned in colour or stamped to harmonize with the metal tracery that is to hold all together . . . Such a city would clean itself in the rain, would know no fire alarms; no, nor any glooms. To any extent the light could be reduced within the rooms by screens, blinds, or insertions of translucent or opaque glass.

In a further paragraph later on in the article Wright refers to the popular demand that existed in the United States of America to rid buildings of walls and posts. He goes on:

Left: Lloyd Wright, Wayfarer's Chapel (National Swedenborg Memorial), Portuguese Bend, California, 1951.

Right: A tower based directly on Constructivist principles; the Empire Tower and Restaurant, Glasgow Exhibition, 1938, by Thomas Tait.

He goes on:

Crystal plates have now quite generally taken the place of fundamental walls and piers in almost all commercial buildings; and glass, the curse of the classic, is a tempting material now about to be explored . . . we have yet to give glass proper architectural recognition.

Wright recognised it in many projects, but his son Lloyd Wright translated it finally into Scheerbartian terms with his Wayfarer's Chapel at Portuguese Bend, California, in 1951.

Today the situation is changed. Many new materials have been introduced that have superseded – in an experimental way at least – the desire for a glass and steel paradise. Ray domes, see-through inflatables, and stretched skin surfaces, which are now possible in translucent plastics, have brought in a new era, and like every revolutionary phase these materials have their poetic protagonists. Buckminster Fuller, who has inspired our own generation, has re-emphasised the role of the visionary and thus echoed the claim of Paul Scheerbart at the turn of the century to transform the world by architecture.

NOTES

[1] See Chapter 50 of *Glass Architecture* for the origin of the idea of an Alpine architecture.

[2] The concept of 'towards', or 'the way to', was incorporated by Le Corbusier into the title of his major publication, *Vers une architecture*, and comes out even clearer in the Etchells translation, *Towards a New Architecture*. It has been used to the point of absolute boredom in magazine articles and publishers' titles ever since. It was not the only term borrowed by Le Corbusier from Bruno Taut: 'Wohnmaschine' (living machine) was another.

[3] Reyner Banham, 'The Glass Paradise', *Architectural Review*, February 1959, pp. 87–9.

[4] Reyner Banham, *The Architecture of the Well Tempered Environment*, London, 1970.

[5] The Crystal Palace fire at Sydenham in 1936 proved Scheerbart wrong on this one.

[6] For a full record of the work of the Glass Chain Group see the exhibition catalogue, *Die gläserne Kette: Visionäre Architekturen aus dem Kreis um Bruno Taut, 1919–20*, Berlin, 1963 and also Chapters 6–8 in Dennis Sharp, *Modern Architecture and Expressionism*, London, 1966.

[7] English translation: Arthur Korn, *Glass in Modern Architecture*, London, 1969.

Glasarchitektur has recently been reissued in German in the Reihe Passagen Series, Rogner & Bernhard, Munich, 1971.

MAJOR PUBLICATIONS BY PAUL SCHEERBART

1889 (1893) *Das Paradies, die Heimat der Kunst.*
1893 *Ja . . . was . . . möchten wir nicht alles! Ein Wunderfabelbuch, Heft I.*
1897 (1900) *Tarub, Bagdads berühmte Köchin. Ein arabischer Kulturroman.*
1897 *Ich liebe Dich! Ein Eisenbahnroman mit 66 Intermezzos.*
1897 *Der Tod der Barmekiden. Arabischer Haremsroman.*
1898 *Na prost! Ein phantastischer Königsroman.*
1900 *Rakkóx, der Billlionär, und die wilde Jagd. Ein Protzenroman und ein Entwicklungsroman in acht anderen Geschichten.*
1901 *Die Seeschlange. Ein Seeroman.*
1902 *Liwûna und Kaidôh. Ein Seelenroman.*
1902 *Die grosse Revolution. Ein Mondroman.*
1902 *Immer mutig! Ein phantastischer Nilpferderoman mit 83 merkwürdigen Geschichten (2 volumes).*
1903 *Kometentanz. Astrale Pantomime.*
1903 *Der Aufgang zur Sonne. Hausmärchen.*
1904 *Machtspässe. Arabische Novellen.*
1904 *Revolutionäre Theater-Bibliothek. (22 plays in 6 volumes.)*
1904 *Der Kaiser von Utopia. Ein Volksroman.*
1904 *Don Miguel de Cervantes Saavedra.*
1906 *Münchhausen und Clarissa. Ein Berliner Roman.*
1907 *Jenseitsgalerie. Ein Mappenwerk.*
1909 *Katerpoesie.*
1909 *Die Entwicklung des Luftmilitarismus und die Auflösung der europäischen Landheere, Festungen und Seeflotten. Eine Flugschrift.*
1910 *Das Perpetuum mobile. Die Geschichte einer Erfindung.*
1912 *Astrale Noveletten.*
1913 *Lesabéndio. Ein Asteroiden-Roman (republished).*
1914 *Das Graue Tuch und zehn Prozent Weiss. Ein Damenroman.*
1914 *Glasarchitektur.*

GLASS ARCHITECTURE

by

Paul Scheerbart

Synopsis of Chapters

1 Environment and its influence on the development of culture

2 The veranda

3 The Botanical Gardens at Dahlem

4 Double glass walls, light, heating and cooling

5 The iron skeleton and the reinforced concrete skeleton

6 The inner framework of glass surfaces

7 The avoidance of wood in furniture and interior decoration

8 The furniture in the middle of the room

9 The larger veranda and its independence of the main building

10 Garden houses and pavilions

11 Stone flags and majolica on garden paths

12 Magnesite and the perfect floor covering for the house

13 The functional style

14 The cladding of building materials and its justification

15 The finishing and plastic treatment of reinforced concrete

16 Enamel and niello applied to metal panels on reinforced concrete

17 Glass fibres in applied art

18 The beauty of the Earth, when glass architecture is everywhere

19 Gothic cathedrals and castles

20 Ancient Greece without glass, the East with ampullæ and majolica tiles

21 Glass, enamel, majolica and porcelain

22 The effects of Tiffany

23 The avoidance of the quicksilver effects of mirrors

24 The avoidance of figure-representation in architecture

25 The landscape architect and the tree and plant world in the Rococo period

26 The door

27 The chair

28 Metal in art and applied art

29 Hollow glass elements in every possible colour and form as a wall material (the so-called 'glass-brick')

30 Aschinger's buildings in Berlin, 1893

31 Glass mosaic and reinforced concrete

32 Heating and cooling appliances in special columns, vases, suspended elements, etc.

33 Lighting between the double walls (which does not exclude suspended fittings in the room)

34 The vacuum-cleaner – in the park, too – also as an insect-exterminator

35 Ventilators, which are ousting the customary windows

36 Light columns and light towers

37 Direction-finding for aeronautics

38 Ukley mother-of-pearl on the concrete wall

39 Wired glass

40 The vertical in architecture, and how to overcome it

41 The developments made possible by iron construction

42 Movable partitions in the home and the park

43 Overcoming the danger of fire

44 Vanquishing vermin

45 Floodlights in the park, on towers and house-roofs

46 Getting rid of the usual illumination effects

47 The end of the window; the loggia and the balcony

48 Stone mosaic as paving

49 Models for glass architecture

50 Mountain illumination

51 Park illumination

52 Ghostly illumination

53 The solid wall as background for sculpture

54 Cars, motor boats and coloured glass

55 The steam and electric railway lit up in colour

56 Nature in another light

57 Reinforced concrete in water

58 Floating architecture

59 River and lake shipping in coloured lighting

60 Aircraft with coloured lights

61 Reinforced concrete and the architecture of fences

62 Terraces

63 View-points

Honi soit qui mal y pense

Dedicated to

BRUNO TAUT

1 Environment and its influence on the development of culture

We live for the most part in closed rooms. These form the environment from which our culture grows. Our culture is to a certain extent the product of our architecture. If we want our culture to rise to a higher level, we are obliged, for better or for worse, to change our architecture. And this only becomes possible if we take away the closed character from the rooms in which we live. We can only do that by introducing glass architecture, which lets in the light of the sun, the moon, and the stars, not merely through a few windows, but through every possible wall, which will be made entirely of glass – of coloured glass. The new environment, which we thus create, must bring us a new culture.

2 The veranda

Obviously the first thing to tackle is something quickly done. To start with, therefore, the veranda can be transformed. It is easy to enlarge it, and to surround it on three sides with double glass walls. Both these walls will be ornamentally coloured and, with the light between them, the effect of the veranda in the evening, inside and out, will be most impressive. If a view of the garden is to be provided, this can be achieved by using transparent window-panes. But it is better not to fit window-type panes. Ventilators are better for admitting air.

In a modest way, it is thus comparatively easy for any villa-owner to create 'glass architecture'. The first step is very simple and convenient.

3 The Botanical Gardens at Dahlem

We already have glass architecture in botanical gardens. The Botanical Gardens at Dahlem near Berlin show that very imposing glass palaces have been erected. But – colour is missing. In the evening sunlight, however, the Palm House and the Cold House look so magnificent that one has a good idea of what could be achieved if colour were exploited. The Palm House is particularly interesting: outside, the seemingly unsupported iron* construction; inside, the framework of wood glazing bars, so that no rust-water accumulates and the iron can be repainted again and again. Wood, because of its impermanence, is not an impressive material. The worst thing, though, is that the glass walls are single and not double; in consequence, the expenditure on winter heating is simply enormous. In one of its guidebooks, the management recounts with unjustified pride that in winter, in a single day with a temperature at 8 am of —10 degrees

* Throughout the translation of *Glasarchitekur* the German word *Eisen* is given as 'iron'.

centigrade, a load of 300 centners* of best Silesian coal is consumed. That, it will be conceded, is rather excessive and not a fit source of pride. Heating expenses of this sort should have been countered with double glass walls.

4 Double glass walls, light, heating and cooling

As air is one of the worst conductors of heat, the double glass wall is an essential condition for all glass architecture. The walls can be a metre apart – or have an even greater space between. The light between these walls shines outward and inward, and both the outer and the inner walls may be ornamentally coloured. If, in so doing, too much light is absorbed by the colour, the external wall may be left entirely clear; it is then advisable simply to provide the light between the walls with a coloured glass shade, so that the wall light in the evening does not dazzle on the outside.

To place heating and incandescent elements between the walls is in most cases not to be recommended, since by this means too much warmth or cold is lost to the outer atmosphere. Heating and cooling elements, however, can be suspended like lamps in the interior, where all hanging lights are to some extent superfluous, since light is distributed by the walls.

In the first instance it is clearly advisable to build glass houses only in the temperate zones, and not in the equatorial and polar regions as well; in the warmer climates one could not do without a white reinforced concrete roof, but in temperate zones this need does not arise. To provide floor heating and cover, electrically-heated carpets are recommended.

5 The iron skeleton and the reinforced concrete skeleton

An iron skeleton is of course indispensable for glass architecture. This will inevitably stimulate an extraordinary upsurge in heavy industry. How to protect iron from rust has not yet been solved in a satisfactory manner. There are many methods of counteracting rust, but so far we do not know which is the best. The simple protective coating, long in vogue, leaves much to be desired æsthetically. The glass architect must surely think of something better to offer. But we can confidently leave this to future developments.

If we are ready to allow larger dimensions to the structural frame, for not every particle of the glass house has to be of glass, a reinforced concrete skeleton is well worth thinking about, for it has proved itself so admirably as a building material, that nothing more need be said about its merits here. Reinforced concrete can also be handled artistically – either with colour or to æsthetic effect by designs cut with the chisel.

* About 15 tons [Ed.].

6 The inner framework of glass surfaces

The iron or reinforced concrete skeleton virtually frames the glass, but the glazed surfaces must have another smaller inner frame. For this purpose in the Botanical Gardens, as already mentioned, impermanent wood was used. Instead of wood a durable material must now be found. Iron is certainly more lasting, but has to be protected against rust, which can be done by nickelling or coating with paint. The latter, as has been said before, is æsthetically displeasing and has to be renewed often. Perhaps reinforced concrete is an ideal building material here, as it does not take up so much surface.

Various other new building materials might be considered, but these have not yet been sufficiently tested for them to be thought of as entirely credible materials suitable for framing glazed surfaces. It is the technical man's problem, and he will surely find the right answer. In any case, only very strong and rust-free materials are potentially appropriate; wood is not durable and in iron constructions should only be used as a last resort. Wood is no longer used in bridges either; they are built entirely of iron and reinforced concrete. Similarly, glass architecture is half-iron architecture. Heavy industry has consequently won a completely new market, which is bound to raise the consumption of iron tenfold.

7 The avoidance of wood in furniture and interior decoration

Inside the glass house, too, wood is to be avoided; it is no longer appropriate. Cupboards, tables and chairs must be made of glass if the whole environment is to convey a sense of unity. This will naturally be a grievous blow to the wood industry. Nickel-steel would, of course, have to be decorated with enamel and niello, so that the furniture may create a striking æsthetic effect – like extremely fine wood-carving and wooden cabinets inlaid with other woods. Wood is to be avoided, because of its impermanence, but the use of iron in iron-glass construction lies along the natural line of development.

8 The furniture in the middle of the room

It will surely appear self-evident that the furniture in the glass house may not be placed against the precious, ornamentally-coloured glass walls. Pictures on the walls are, of course, totally impossible. Given the highest intentions, this revolution in the environment is inevitable. Glass architecture will have a tough fight on its hands, but force of habit must be overcome. Ideas derived from our grandparents must no longer be the deciding influence in the new environment. Everything new has to wage an arduous campaign against entrenched tradition. It cannot be otherwise, if the new is to prevail.

9 The larger veranda and its independence of the main building

Whoever has provided his veranda with colour-ornamented glass on three sides will soon want to have more glass architecture. One thing leads to another, and to stop the process is unthinkable. So the veranda continues to grow; in the end it emancipates itself from the main building, and may become the main building itself. To promote this evolution of the veranda will be the chief task of every glass architect.

10 Garden houses and pavilions

The ancient Arabs lived far more in their gardens than in their castles. For this reason garden houses and kiosks were very quickly developed by them. Unluckily, since perishable wood was their constant choice of building material, nothing remains of this Arabian garden architecture.

The task of the modern architect, therefore, is to use only the best iron and reinforced concrete materials for garden houses and pavilions, and to encourage double colour-ornamented glass walls everywhere in the garden. In introducing glass architecture, it is best to begin with the garden; every owner of a large garden will want to have a glass garden house.

11 Stone flags and majolica on garden paths

In their gardens, the Arabs had patterned floors of stone and majolica; they thus transferred their taste for carpets to their gardens. The Dutch have copied this from the Arabs.

Modern glass architects will be well advised to pave their garden paths with stone and majolica tiles, for in this way the splendour of the glass palaces will be worthily framed.

12 Magnesite and the perfect floor covering for the house

We can now hardly avoid considering many new building materials, but only by way of suggestion. Jointless magnesite floors have much to recommend them; but whether they are equally suited to the house, with its colourful glass walls, is not so easily decided. In any case, many other materials obviously come into the picture as the perfect floor covering – even stone 'parquet', consisting of stones arranged like mosaic. But magnesite should be very durable, and therefore good. Inside the house one will have to be sparing with colour for the floor, in order to achieve a contrasting effect with the walls.

13 The functional style

The reader might gain the impression that glass architecture is rather cold, but in warm weather, coolness is not unpleasant. Anyhow, let me make it clear that colours in glass can produce a most glowing effect, shedding perhaps a new warmth. What has been said up to now takes on a somewhat warmer atmosphere. I should like to resist most vehemently the undecorated 'functional style',* for it is inartistic. It has often been adopted before in other contexts, and this is happening once again.

For a transition period, the functional style seems to me acceptable; at all events it has done away with imitations of older styles, which are simply products of brick architecture and wooden furniture. Ornamentation in the glass house will evolve entirely of its own accord – the oriental decoration, the carpets and the majolica will be so transformed that in glass architecture we shall never, I trust, have to speak of copying. At least, let's hope so!

14 The cladding of building materials and its justification

A housefront faced with perishable plaster is clearly reprehensible, and a single coat of paint, which is not weather-proof, is obviously not permissible. Architects have therefore declared any cladding unjustifiable and display the brick front completely naked. A ghastly sight! Brick is only effective if it has weathered and has the character of a ruin – when it looks like a ruin. The ancient Egyptians faced their brick pyramids with smooth granite slabs. These have not been destroyed, but stolen. If the latter occurs, preservation is naturally out of the question. A cladding of an inferior material is, in my opinion, fully justified.

Since, nowadays, there are very many buildings which cannot be replaced in a day by glass structures, we may reasonably give some thought to durable facing materials for factories, harbour installations, etc. Enamelled panels of iron and majolica are particularly suitable. Old walls, brick 'fences', stables, and so on, can be clad in this way.

Houses, too, can be given a passable veneer with roof-gardens, if large numbers of glass pavilions are erected in them.

15 The finishing and plastic treatment of reinforced concrete

Reinforced concrete is a building material which is very strong and weather-resistant. It has been rightly acclaimed by architects as the ideal material. A pity that it is not transparent: only glass is.

* The German word here is '*Sachstil*' (author's quotes) [Ed.].

But reinforced concrete is unsightly if left in its natural state. A smooth finish to reinforced concrete, which is perfectly feasible, is therefore much to be recommended; the finish should also be able to take weather-proof colour. In addition, reinforced concrete should be provided with plastic decoration; it is as easy to work with the chisel as granite.

Granite is not exactly easy to work, but it can be done.

16 Enamel and niello applied to metal panels on reinforced concrete

If thin metal panels can be pressed into the surface of reinforced concrete during casting, these can be given an enamel coating – possibly one of transparent *cloisonné* enamel.* Small surfaces can also be hollowed out and filled with niello,† although lacquered niello is only suitable for interiors. Externally, metal niello would be very effective, but only precious metals should be used; the patina of bronze would also be suitable. Glass mosaic, too, is an obvious possibility.

17 Glass fibres in applied art

It has been forgotten by many that glass can be developed as fibres which can be spun. The story goes back more than forty years, perhaps further. I am not sure. These glass fibres may lead to a whole new industry in applied art; divan covers, chair arms, etc., can be made of them.

18 The beauty of the Earth, when glass architecture is everywhere

The face of the earth would be much altered if brick architecture were ousted everywhere by glass architecture. It would be as if the earth were adorned with sparkling jewels and enamels. Such glory is unimaginable. All over the world it would be as splendid as in the gardens of the Arabian Nights. We should then have a paradise on earth, and no need to watch in longing expectation for the paradise in heaven.

19 Gothic cathedrals and castles

Glass architecture is unthinkable without Gothic. In the days when Gothic cathedrals and castles were rising, an architecture of glass was also tried. It was

* A pattern of raised metal strips, filled in with transparent enamel.
† A black compound worked into a pattern cut into the surface.

not completely realised, because iron, the indispensable material, was not yet available, and this alone enables the totally glass room to be constructed. In Gothic times, glass was entirely unknown in most private houses. Today it is a principal factor in the architecture of every house. But it still lacks colour. Colour, however, will come.

20 Ancient Greece without glass, the East with ampullae and majolica tiles

In ancient Greece glass was almost unknown. But before the Hellenic civilisation there were already many colourful glass ampullae and lustrous majolica tiles in the countries bordering the Euphrates and Tigris, a thousand years before Christ. The Near East is thus the so-called cradle of glass culture.

21 Glass, enamel, majolica and porcelain

All building materials which are durable and obtainable in weather-resistant colours, have the right to be used. Brittle brick and inflammable wood have no such right; a brick building is also easy to shatter by explosives, which endanger the whole building equally. This is not the case in a glass-iron building; only partial destruction can be induced by explosives in the latter.

Wherever the use of glass is impossible, enamel, majolica and porcelain can be employed, which at least can display durable colour, even if they are not translucent like glass.

22 The effects of Tiffany

The famous American Tiffany, who introduced the 'Tiffany glass', has by this means greatly stimulated the glass industry; he put coloured clouds into glass. With these clouds the most marvellous effects are feasible – and the walls acquire an entirely new charm, which admittedly puts the decoration into the background, but in particular situations is quite practicable.

23 The avoidance of the quicksilver effects of mirrors

If the dangers of Tiffany effects may not be wholly ignored – they are only dangerous, after all, in inartistic hands – one should only allow the quicksilver effects of mirrors a utilitarian existence in the dressing-room. In the other rooms of the house mirror-effects, which continue to reflect their surroundings again and again in a different light, disturb the general architectural impression, for they do not last. When kaleidoscopic effects are wanted, they are perfectly justified. Otherwise it is best to do without the quicksilver-mirror; for it is dangerous – like poison.

24 The avoidance of figure representation in architecture

While architecture is spatial art, figure-representation is not spatial art and has no place in architecture. The animal and human body is made for movement. Architecture is not made for movement, and is concerned with formal composition and ornament. Only the plant and mineral kingdoms should be exploited – better still the whole repertoire of free invention – one should not think of the animal and human body as a design element. The fact that the ancient Egyptians did so is no reason at all for doing so today; we no longer associate our gods with the bodies of animals and humans.

25 The landscape architect and the tree and plant world in the Rococo period

The Rococo period treated trees and plants as if they were mouldable clay; to create perspective effects trees were shaped like walls and yew hedges clipped into geometrical figures. At the same time, the architect ruled the garden, which he should do today. But such laborious treatment of plant and tree material does not pay – because of the changing seasons and transitory results.

More glass walls in the garden would give it quite a different aspect, linking the garden to the architecture of the house, if the latter is glass architecture. It is scarcely imaginable what wonderful effects could be achieved in this way. An occasional mirror-wall close to pools is worth considering. But not too many.

26 The door

In our technical age developments occur rapidly; we often forget this. There is no reason to think that they will suddenly slow down. Fifty years ago there was not a single town in Germany with main water and drainage. Fifty years later one cannot imagine a home without a vacuum cleaner. And there will be many other things which now strike us as utopian, although those which are now feasible, like glass architecture, should never be so described.

The door in the glass house, for example, will be unlike those most commonly found today in brick houses. Self-closing doors are commonplace nowadays, but self-opening doors will be equally common soon. The outside doors do not need to open by themselves, but if the inside ones are self-opening, it is like a friendly gesture by the householder, although he does not have to make any movement with his hands. The mechanism is actuated by treading quite lightly on a sensitive plate. It already exists in Berlin pubs, and has been fully worked out and patented. The idea can be extended; rotating crystal elements – or flashing lights – can be set in motion in doors; a friendlier greeting than that of a liveried supercilious servant.

The doors can be made of transparent glass with crystal effects, and of ornamentally coloured glasses. To every room, then, its own particular entrance. This should create a more festive atmosphere. The outside doors can also be of glass.

Cities in their present form are not yet fifty years old. They can vanish as quickly as they came. Even the permanent way of the steam railway is not immortal.

27 The chair

The most complicated item in the whole of applied art is the chair. The steel chair seems to be an æsthetic impossibility, yet steel can be made so splendid with enamel and niello that it need not fear comparison with the finest Venetian carving. The prices of enamel and niello chairs are far from being higher than carved wood chairs, for which 4-500 marks are willingly paid. Enamel work is so cheap that enamelled chairs can be produced very well for 100 marks apiece.

Of course, an industry which turns out identical chairs by the score will have to be disregarded. But one can reasonably expect that an industry which wants to satisfy artistic requirements will stop the indiscriminate production of identical objects.

The industry of the future will also turn eagerly to glass fibres. For only fire-resistant materials will be used – both for divans and for flooring, where glass fibres will prove the most important material.

28 Metal in art and applied art

It seems to me that habit lies like a heavy lead weight upon art and applied art. Because in grandfather's time most furniture and artefacts were made of wood, they must continue to be made of wood. But this should not be so. Glass architecture is also a compelling influence on applied art and art in general. We shall therefore be obliged to give preference in all fields to metal. The æstheticians will naturally try to counteract this, and the threatened timber industry will mobilise them.

There will be a lot of talk about the valuable associative ideas inherent in wood. I believe, however, that all the associative ideas inherent in wood can be transmitted to metal – by developing the artistic potentialities of metal – as I have already indicated many times. Metal is supposed to be cold, whereas wood is supposed to be warm. These are notions born of habit: we found glazed tiles cold before the existence of the tiled stove. Majolica only became warm to us because of this association. The same thing may occur with metal.

29 Hollow glass elements in every possible colour and form as a wall material (the so-called 'glass-brick')

So-called glass bricks make a wall material which may well become an interesting speciality of glass architecture. Large industrial undertakings have been formed already which could have a big future. Everything fire-proof and transparent is æsthetically justifiable as a wall material. Glass bricks should make many iron skeletons superfluous.

30 Aschinger's buildings in Berlin, 1893

If ideas are to be productive, they must really be 'in the air' – in very many heads at the same time – even if in a distorted form. This became clear to me in 1893 or a little later. Franz Evers was editing the theosophist journal *Sphinx*, and in consequence was overwhelmed with theosophist, spiritualist and other such literature; in this wilderness there was a lot to make one laugh. One gentleman, whose name escapes me, asserted that glass was the source of all salvation; that one must always have a glass crystal near one on the writing-table, and sleep in a room of mirrors, etc., etc. It all sounded crazy. But Aschinger's beer halls, with their frightful mirrors, seemed to me an echo of that theosophist publication about mirrored bedrooms. At any rate some telepathic influence was at work.

I am convinced that every constructive idea will appear in many heads at the same time and quite irrationally; one should therefore not speak carelessly about the seemingly confused and crazy; it generally contains the germ of reason.

In the East the madman is left at liberty and honoured as a prophet. But that is by the way.

31 Glass mosaic and reinforced concrete

It must be emphasised that reinforced concrete with a glass mosaic skin is probably the most durable building material which we have so far discovered. People are always so afraid that glass may be shattered by some malicious hand.

Now, cases of windows being broken by stones thrown from the street are probably infrequent nowadays; stones are far more often thrown at a man's head than at a window-pane. But I have never heard of stones being thrown at glass mosaic.

During the last century, when telegraph wires were introduced, it was thought that they should all be laid underground for fear of the rude populace. Today nobody thinks of destroying the overhead wires.

Therefore there is no need to fear that glass houses would be destroyed by stones flung by the lower orders.

But that, too, is by the way.

32 Heating and cooling appliances in special columns, vases, suspended elements, etc.

Although the electric light commands the room from between the double walls, this is not the place for the heating and cooling because, as already stated, half the warmth and cold air is uselessly dissipated.

For this reason the heating can be installed in columns, vases and suspended elements, and their outer shells can be designed, like the oriental ampulla, as delightful decoration.

33 Lighting between the double walls (which does not exclude suspended fittings in the room)

I have so often said that the double walls are there, not merely to maintain the temperature of the room, but to accommodate the lighting elements. I must ask to be forgiven for repetition but I want to stress and underline it.

With this type of lighting the whole glass house becomes a big lantern which, on peaceful summer and winter nights, shines like fire-flies and glow-worms. One could easily become poetic. But lighting can also be installed inside the room. This interior lighting also illuminates the walls – if not so strongly as the light between the double walls.

34 The vacuum– cleaner – in the park, too – also as insect – exterminator

In the near future the vacuum-cleaner will seem as important as main water, and it will be used in parks, for the inlaid paths must be kept free of 'dust'. The vacuum-cleaner will naturally be needed as an insect-exterminator. It is absolutely horrifying that today it is still not used for this purpose. That the vacuum-cleaner has already been employed for getting rid of street dust, I take to be a known fact.

35 Ventilators, which are ousting the customary windows

It will seem very natural that ventilators should have a principal part to play in a glass house, and will supplant everything window-like. When I am in my glass room, I shall hear and see nothing of the outside world. If I long for the sky, the clouds, woods and meadows, I can go out or repair to an extra-veranda with transparent glass panes.

36 Light columns and light towers

Hitherto, columns have served only as supports. Iron construction needs fewer supports than masonry; most of them are superfluous in the glass house. In order to make the columns in larger glass buildings lighter, they can be equipped with light elements behind a completely glass surround, so that the light columns do not give the impression of supporting, and the entire architectural effect seems much more free – as if everything were self-supporting; glass architecture will acquire an almost floating quality with these light columns.

Towns and other places should always be distinguished by towers. Every effort must naturally be made to lend enchantment to towers by night. Under the rule of glass architecture, therefore, all towers must become towers of light.

37 Direction-finding for aeronautics

Aeronautics will undoubtedly be determined to conquer the night. All towers must therefore become towers of light. And – to simplify navigation – every light tower will be built differently, emit a different light, and be fitted with glass elements of widely differing form. Uniformity in light towers is consequently out of the question. The signalling impulse can be so simple, and the tower itself must be so different from any other, that the aeronaut will immediately be informed where he is.

38 Ukley mother-of-pearl on the concrete wall

Naturally, transparent walls are not possible everywhere, in particular because the householder may not always want to sit or lie down between transparent walls. For such rooms, however, wallpapers and wall-fabrics are to be avoided because of fire risks, and wood-panelling is no longer appropriate – it is as impermanent as paper and fabrics, encourages woodworm and is potentially inflammable.

Another wall cladding material must now be found. Reinforced concrete is not easy to handle artistically; it is as hard as granite, and enamel and niello are not all that cheap, anyway. Imitation pearls are coated with Ukley mother-of-pearl. This coating is perhaps to be recommended for walls as well. It could easily be embellished with semi-precious stones and glass brilliants.

But it is quite possible that a mother-of-pearl coat, applied to an uneven surface, could do the job alone. Whether this artificial mother-of-pearl retains its colour when daylight is kept away from it would have to be tested.

Dome-like undulating bulges may be very effective if they occur regularly and symmetrically.

39 Wired glass

For the walls, a good glass material is still, of course, the most worthwhile. After glass mosaic, however, the most durable glass material is the fairly familiar wired glass, which is particularly suitable for the external wall. Nowadays, wired glass can be handled in such a way that the wire mesh is scarcely visible. In the external wall the mesh does not matter because to an outside viewer it is practically invisible.

40 The vertical in architecture, and how to overcome it

The brick architecture of the past often overcame the problem of the vertical by domes, but to escape from the vertical in walls seemed impossible. In glass architecture it is quite different. The large Palm House in the Botanical Gardens in Berlin no longer has vertical walls; the upward curve begins at a height of three metres.

41 The developments made possible by iron construction

Iron construction permits walls of any desired form. Vertical walls are no longer inevitable. The developments made possible by iron construction are thus quite unlimited. One can shift the overhead dome effects to the sides, so that, sitting at a table, one only has to glance up sideways to appreciate them. Curved surfaces are also effective for the lower parts of walls – it is specially easy to get results in smaller rooms which are even less tied to verticals. The importance of the ground-plan in architecture will be reduced by such means; the building's silhouette will now be more significant than it used to be.

42 Movable partitions in the home and the park

The Japanese constantly changes his living space by dividing it into smaller areas by partition-screens. Different silk materials are laid over these screens from time to time, so that the smaller 'room' can have a frequently varying appearance. The same can be done in the living-rooms of glass houses by mobile and sliding glass partitions.

If one introduces movable glass walls, which of course do not have to be vertical, into a park, one can create wonderful perspectives, and a very delicate architecture of higher wall-screens could give the park a new architectural significance. This novelty would be perpetually flexible.

43 Overcoming the danger of fire

After what has been said, it is probably obvious that glass architecture makes fire-protection superfluous. By avoiding all inflammable materials fire insurance can be abolished. But the exclusion of fire risks should always be born in mind in architecture; in the applied arts and interior decoration, only materials which do not burn should be permitted.

44 Vanquishing vermin

That in a glass house, if properly built, vermin must be unknown, needs no further comment.

45 Floodlights in the park, on towers and house-roofs

As coloured glass greatly softens the strength of light, we have far too little electric light at the present time. But we should have a thousand times as much, if, wherever there is running water, we installed turbines, as is feasible. Given adequate light, we can have far more floodlights than before, and night can become day. The night, indeed, can be more glorious than the day, quite independently of the splendour of the starlit sky, which, when it is clouded, is invisible to us anyway.

Even the private citizen will have his 'park' flood-lit, and there will be floodlights on all roof constructions and roof-gardens. And a tower without floodlights will then be entirely unfamiliar and look unnatural. Aeronauts will show their indignation at unlit towers.

46 Getting rid of the usual illumination effects

Glass architecture will be scornfully called 'illuminations architecture' by its opponents, who naturally should not be ignored. This contempt is unjustifiable, for nobody will want to illuminate a glass house the way a brick house is lit up today; when it is lighted inside the glass house is in itself an illumination element. When there are many such elements, the effect cannot be so harsh as the primitive elements of present-day illumination. By manipulating mobile reflectors, the floodlights can project a thousand beams of every conceivable colour into the sky. Mirrors (used with discretion) and floodlights together will oust the usual illumination. The new illumination will be essentially for airship travel, to guide the aeronaut.

47 The end of the window; the loggia and the balcony

With the introduction of electricity for cooking and heating, the chimney must unquestionably be abolished. People claim that such an introduction would be expensive, but forget that the tempo of technical development is continually quickening. Admittedly, this happens in the workshop and the expert's room, where talking a lot about oneself is frowned upon. But the enthusiasm is no less.

When glass architecture comes in, there will not be much more talk of windows either; the word 'window' will disappear from the dictionaries. Whoever wants to look at nature can go on to his balcony or into his loggia, which of course can be arranged for enjoying nature as before. But then it will not be spoilt by hideous brick houses.

These are visions of the future, which we must none the less keep in mind, if the new age is ever to come about.

48 Stone mosaic as paving

Up to now, we have not adequately discussed how to pave the surface underfoot. Stone flags are recommended for all paths and paved areas in gardens, but inside the house only magnesite has been mentioned for floors, in rooms of secondary importance. For better rooms, stone mosaic alone is advisable. Of course, the colours of the floor must be made to match the glass walls or to contrast with them. Perhaps a fibre-glass carpet would also be practicable. But inflammable materials must be rejected, and carpets of materials not fire-proofed, even if this is difficult.

49 Models for glass architecture

The most important objective would be for a number of models of glass architecture to be exhibited. Let us hope this happens at the 1914 Werkbund Exhibition at Cologne, for which Bruno Taut has built a glass house, in which the entire glass industry is to be represented. It does not seem right to me to produce models of glass architecture of pasteboard and selenite, but brass and glass models would not be cheap. A new model-building industry ought to be created to make models only for glass architecture, including church buildings, from good materials. Perhaps it would be advisable to use a different imitation-glass for larger models. About twenty years ago there was a substance called Tektorium – it was a transparent, coloured, leather-like material on wire-netting. For model purposes it would be admirable, but for buildings it would not be durable enough, although it could always be mended.

50 Mountain illumination

So much sounds fantastic, which actually is not fantastic at all. If one suggests applying mountain illumination to the Himalayas, this is just a ridiculous fantasy outside the realms of practical discussion. Illuminating the mountains near the Lake of Lugano is quite another thing. There are so many hotels there which would like to be part of the scenery, that they would be well disposed to glass architecture, if the proposition were not beyond their means. Their means are not inconsiderable, and the illumination of the mountains by illuminating the hotels, if these were built of glass, can no longer be described as fantastic. The rack-railway, which ascends the Rigi, could also be illuminated very easily and effectively by flood-lights.

When aeronautics have conquered the dark, the whole of Switzerland will have her mountains colourfully lit up at night by glass architecture.

We constantly forget how many things have changed in the last century. In the 1830s the aged Goethe did not see the coming of the railways. Less than a hundred years have passed since then, and the whole earth is encompassed by steel rails. Mountain illumination, which today still seems a fantasy to many, can develop just as quickly.

51 Park illumination

But park illumination will develop sooner than mountain illumination. If only we have more electric light, much will evolve of its own accord. Above all, we should consider towers of various forms in the parks for guiding airships (as already discussed).

A glass tower should not only be equipped with flood-lights; many of the glass surfaces could be made to move and so bring about kaleidoscopic effects. Here also the possibilities are boundless.

52 Ghostly illumination

When we speak of light, we are generally thinking of the glaring light of gas and electricity. In the past fifty years light has progressed quite surprisingly. It is all happening so quickly that one can hardly keep up. But if we had light in greater quantity (and this is perfectly feasible by using more turbines and dynamos), it would not have to be harsh in its effect and could be softened by colour. It can be so reduced by colour that it looks ghostly, which to many people would perhaps seem sympathetic.

53 The solid wall as background for sculpture

Where one either cannot or will not remove a solid non-transparent wall, it may perhaps be suitable as background for plastic art. This need not be statuary. Ornamental work stands out very effectively against a wall, and plant motifs are also simple to apply. But painting should not be used. In any case, it detracts from the architectural unity of a building.

54 Cars, motor boats and coloured glass

Now let us transfer glass architecture to the world of movement – to cars and motor boats. In this way the landscape will become quite different; it has already been permanently transformed by the steam train – so transformed that for decades people could not grow used to the change. The coloured automobile, with its glossy glazed surfaces, and the glass motor boat, however, will alter the landscape so pleasantly that mankind, let us hope, should adjust itself to the change more quickly.

55 The steam and electric railway lit up in colour

When glass architecture has once successfully captured the car and the motor boat, there will naturally be no course open to the other vehicles, especially those which scorch along rails, except to accommodate themselves to it. We shall then enjoy a wonderful impression, if we see an express illuminated in colour speeding by day or by night through the countryside. The railway, greeted so sourly by sensitive natures to start with, will in the end reach a level of artistic charm beyond our present powers of description.

56 Nature in another light

After the introduction of glass architecture, the whole of nature in all cultural regions will appear to us in quite a different light. The wealth of coloured glass is bound to give nature another hue, as if a new light were shed over the entire natural world. There will be no need to look at nature through a coloured piece of glass. With all this coloured glass everywhere in buildings, and in speeding cars and air- and water-craft, so much new light will undoubtedly emanate from the glass colours that we may well be able to claim that nature appears in another light.

57 Reinforced concrete in water

Reinforced concrete, as is well known, has proved itself in water; it is practically indestructible. It is therefore suitable for a new Venice, which must have foundations that are non-transparent, stable, rust-free and indestructible. Upon this sound base the most colourful glass architecture can rise and be reflected in the water. A new Venice in this style will eclipse the old one. Water, because of its intrinsic capacity to reflect, belongs to glass architecture; the two are almost inseparable, so that in future water will be introduced wherever there is none at the moment. If, after the example of the old Venice, a 'colony' were to be laid out with canal-streets, the traditional Venetian façade-architecture would have to be renounced from the outset; it does not agree with glass buildings which, when they are to be several storeys high, have in any case to be built in pyramid shape with terraces; otherwise too few of the glass walls come in contact with the daylight.

Should the individual sites be very close to one another, care must be taken over suitable boundaries. These can be walls of reinforced concrete, perhaps sheltering a covered way, open on one side. But they could be made in plenty of other ways.

Anyone can develop the theme further, even a non-architect.

58 Floating architecture

If reinforced concrete, as has often been asserted in many quarters – even by the State Material-testing Commission* – cannot be attacked by water, then it is capable of carrying the largest building, like a ship. We can talk in all seriousness of floating architecture. For this, of course, everything which was said in the previous chapter holds good. The buildings can obviously be juxtaposed or moved apart in ever changing patterns, so that every floating town could look different each day. The floating town could swim around in regions of large lakes – perhaps in the sea too. It sounds most fantastic and utopian, but it is far from being so, if reinforced concrete, shaped to the form of an indestructible vessel, carries the architecture. Indestructible boats have already been built out of reinforced concrete in German New Guinea. We must learn to accept that new building materials, when they really are of unrivalled strength and free from rust, can guide the architecture of the whole world into new paths. Reinforced concrete is one such material.

59 River and lake shipping in coloured lighting

As soon as there is floating glass architecture, ships – both great and small – will be fitted out in glass. The rivers, lakes and seas will then become very gay. It does not take much perspicacity to predict this development in lake and river shipping, once a floating building is erected and is imitated.

60 Aircraft with coloured lights

It is generally known that the aeronauts would like to take over the night. That they have not so far done so is easily explained; on the earth the night is not yet light enough. But when, thanks to glass architecture, it has become light down below, it will also be light up in the air; the aircraft will be equipped to project coloured lights, which will also form the vocabulary of a signal-language, understood everywhere by the light-projecting stations of the earth-towers and giving a practical value to the colour display both above and below. Here the elements of progress fit smoothly together and are slowly but steadily completely transforming life on the surface of the earth. The changes brought about by the steam train have not been so significant and far-reaching as those which glass and iron construction is bound to produce. The crucial factor in this is undoubtedly reinforced concrete.

* The German here is *staatliche Materialprufungskommission* [Ed.].

61 Reinforced concrete and the architecture of fences

Reinforced concrete can be a few centimetres thick, and is very convenient to use for fences. If it is treated artistically, with enamel and glass mosaic or embellished with niello ornamentation, areas with such concrete boundary fences can easily be converted into places of recreation.

In the architecture of fences reinforced concrete has a great part to play.

62 Terraces

In higher glass buildings, when there are several storeys, the terrace-form is beyond question a necessity, for otherwise the glazed surfaces do not touch the sunlit air but can only fulfil their purpose at night and not by day. These terrace-form storeys will naturally oust the tedious façade-architecture of brick houses.

63 View-points

One imagines the view-points, from which nowadays we can survey a town or landscape. These view-points will show us quite different pictures, when glass architecture has become general and all vehicles (even the flying ones) reveal the full possibilities of coloured glass. One must simply try to make such view-points clear to visualise. It is not easy, but the imagination soon adapts itself in the end to giving more than isolated details.

64 Glass in factory buildings

To have a comprehensive picture of the glass-architecture world, it is essential also to think of factory buildings in glass. There will be no question of immediately destroying brick structures everywhere, but at first the brick will be faced with glass materials and glazes – and glass garden pavilions will be put on roofs, etc.

65 Market halls entirely of glass and iron

It is well known that market halls are already being built entirely of glass and iron. Missing only are the double walls and ornamental colour. It is not fanciful, however, to assume that both these will come soon. A total architecture of glass and iron cannot be far off.

66 Churches and temples

In Europe the larger church buildings are very well planned and executed as a result of the unnatural concentration of people in the larger towns. Whether it will be possible in this field to impose a purely glass and iron architecture in individual cases by rejecting brick, I do not know. But I do know well that the greater cheapness of glass and iron building must help towards success; we shall only have this greater cheapness when a larger number of firms are in competition – and for that we must wait. The free churches of America may well be the first to build glass temples, thus making a good step forward for glass architecture in the religious sphere.

It ought to be stressed here that the whole of glass architecture stems from the Gothic cathedrals. Without them it would be unthinkable; the Gothic cathedral is the prelude.

67 Club and sports buildings

Club and sports buildings are today being erected in large numbers. As these are almost always the concern of well-to-do societies, glass architects would do well to pay closer attention to them; the advantages of glass architecture for rooms mainly used for social occasions are obvious.

68 Militarism and brick architecture

So often only the obnoxious side of militarism is alluded to; but there is also a good one. It consists in the fact that, with the significant advent of the 'dirigible' aerial torpedo, it inevitably draws attention to the dangers of brick architecture; if a brick church tower is struck low down by a torpedo, it will in every case collapse, kill many people and reduce an entire group of buildings to rubble.

If, therefore, militarism evolves logically, it is bound to bring our brick culture into disrepute; this is its good side, and one constantly emphasised, especially by those tired of living as 'brick-dwellers'. A glass tower, when it is supported by more than four metal piers, will not be destroyed by an aerial torpedo; a few iron members will be bent, and a number of glass panels will have holes or cracks, but such damage is simple to repair.

69 Parliament buildings

What has just been said about glass towers applies also to parliament buildings built entirely of steel and glass. In wartime these, too, are much more resistant to damage than the old parliament buildings of brick faced with sandstone. To many this claim will seem very paradoxical, but it is quite logical. Dynamite can only damage a glass house partially; in relation to the whole it is fairly harmless. It needs a hailstorm of dynamite bombs to destroy a larger building complex made of glass and iron.

70 Restaurants, cafés, hotels and sanatoria

It seems to me beyond question that restaurants, cafés and hotels will be the first to show an interest in glass architecture, in order to attract a larger public, who always have plenty to spend on anything new. Sanatoria also will want glass buildings; the influence of splendid glass architecture on the nerves is indisputable.

71 Transportable buildings

Transportable glass buildings can be produced as well. They are particularly suitable for exhibition purposes. Transportable buildings of this type are not easy to make.

But one must not forget that, in a new movement, the most difficult step is often the first.

72 The future inventor, and the materials which could compete with glass

To earn a lot of money by inventions is not exactly easy. All the same, as I am bound to concede at once, the number of inventors grows daily; while many inventors lose all their goods and chattels and achieve nothing, the others are not deterred. Despite everything, however, the amply provided inventor is, in the long run, a very rare exception. Failure has its humorous side, and, so long as this is so, things are not so bad. But that is by the way. Nevertheless, it cannot be doubted that inventors – for their number, as we have said, is constantly growing – could or should have a great future.

Materials will be invented able to compete with glass. I am thinking of those which are elastic, like rubber, and transparent. The previously mentioned Tektorium is one already invented; but it is only too easily broken – and that, after all, is a defect. However, the outcome may be different. Materials may be invented combining transparency with durability. With the ever-increasing number of inventors everything possible is indeed ultimately possible.

73 The timelessness of ornamental glass and glass mosaic

Meanwhile, since we do not yet have the better, we must put up with the good, and this good is glass and ornamental glass mounted in lead, glass mosaic, and enamel. These glorious materials have not been outmoded by time; they have survived hundreds and thousands of years. It is regrettable that they have not been protected from infamous hands, but tough granite, which was used to face Egyptian pyramids, has fared no better, and has also been stolen.

But this is no place for lamentations; our hope is that glass architecture will also improve mankind in ethical respects. It seems to me that this is a principal merit of lustrous, colourful, mystical and noble glass walls. This quality appears to me not just an illusion, but something very real; the man who sees the splendours of glass every day cannot have ignoble hands.

74 Exhibition buildings in America and Europe

In the past twenty years we in Europe have frequently heard fabulous tales of American glass buildings. In part, these have certainly been only the idle fancies of reporters, but there may well be a grain of truth in them. Tiffany plays a great part in America, and the Americans are very well disposed to glass things. It would be very interesting to know what is planned in glass for the World Exhibition of 1915 in San Francisco.

In my opinion the exhibition buildings in America must differ considerably from those in Europe. The American bridge constructions at Niagara Falls are at all events so magnificent that an exhibition hall, if it is built of iron and glass, should also reveal impressive dimensions. Whether it will be double-walled with coloured decoration, we do not yet know.

America is also the chief country for impressive giant buildings: the Pan-American Railroad, which is intended to protect the North and South against military attacks from East and West, is at present probably the greatest engineering work on earth.

A hope lies here that America might also tackle the greatest architectural work on earth. May it be composed of iron with glass of every colour.

Europe is too conservative and slow.

75 Experimental site for glass architecture

Glass-painters never fix the glass pieces with lead, without first testing the effect experimentally. This is done with all new designs. The full effect cannot be appreciated in the imagination. For the same reason, experiment is also essential for glass buildings. We need an experimental site for the purpose. It would be advisable for such a site to be provided by private enterprise rather than by the state. The latter brings in its official architects, who unhappily are rarely artists and are incapable of becoming so overnight.

76 A permanent exhibition of glass architecture

A glass architecture exhibition would have to be linked to the experimental site, and it would have to be permanent. Glass architecture can only be effectively promoted if every new idea can be exhibited at the same time, and all those interested can constantly order or buy on the spot whatever is best or newest.

77 The crystal room illuminated by translucent floors

At the exhibition, particular attention would have to be given to lighting tests. We do not yet know, for example, what the effect would be of a room lit by translucent floors. One could discuss lights for ever, but things like flooring, and many other ideas, would have to be tested. In my view a Glass Building Association would have to make capital available for the site and exhibition. If the interest were general, the association would soon be formed.

78 Metal filigree with enamel inlay hung in front of crude reinforced concrete

Many experiments could be imagined; the choice is almost unlimited. Particular thought must be given to overcoming the crudeness of reinforced concrete: filigree ornament with enamel inlay is perhaps worth considering. It would look like a piece of jewellery, on a large scale. Much of glass architecture concerns the jeweller, and jewels should be transposed from necks and arms on to walls.

For the time being, ladies are not going to allow this because they are afraid of losing their share of adornment. It is one of the most unpleasant things about many new movements, that the first thing everybody asks is: can it be harmful to me? The old fear of competition is in all things a far from pleasant phenomenon, even in art. The oil-colour manufacturers are undoubtedly opponents of glass-painting, because they cannot make anything out of it.

79 The aeronaut's house with airship models on the roof

Let's turn to something pleasanter! In my opinion, air-navigation will be eager to build an aeronaut's house in the restaurant garden of the exhibition, with airship models projecting little mobile lights fixed to the domed roof. This would be a variant of the *Seeschifferhaus* at Bremen. To immortalise aircraft models in this way would be of great interest to the aeronautical profession, and would lie very close to its heart.

80 Soft lighting

It must be repeated that efforts should not be directed towards achieving greater brightness in lighting, for we have got that already. We should think all the time of the softening of light in choosing colours.

81 Twilight effects

Incidentally, we should consider introducing light behind coloured glass panels into a few corners, even in bright sunshine. It produces wonderful twilight effects during the dusk and dawn hours. A great many lighting experiments will, of course, be necessary.

82 Lighthouses and shipping

When new lighthouses have to be built, the glass architect must see to it that in the immediate future glass architecture is adopted on a large scale. Since lighthouses generally stand on high eminences, it is undoubtedly cheaper than designs in brick, where the frightful labour of lifting such materials to the site disqualifies them. Building will unquestionably be cheaper with the simple equipment needed for carrying up metal and glass. This must be repeatedly emphasised.

83 Airports as glass palaces

For the building of airports, also, glass-iron construction has much to recommend it; airports must be visible and identifiable from far off and this is best achieved by coloured ornamental glass. This will reach its full effect at night, when the entire building is crowned by a diadem of projected lights, delighting not only the aeronauts, but also people who have no airship at their bidding.

84 Light nights, when glass architecture comes

It seems easy to say that something is indescribable, but of those light nights, which glass architecture must bring us, there is nothing else left for us to say except that they are truly indescribable. One thinks of the lights shining from all the glass towers and in every aircraft, and one thinks of these lights in all their many colours. One thinks of the railway trains all gaily lighted, and one adds the factories in which at night, too, the light shines through coloured panes. Then one thinks of the great palaces and cathedrals of glass and the villas of glass, and of the town-like structures, on solid land and in the water – often in movement – and of ever more water in ever different colours. On Venus and Mars they will stare in wonder and no longer recognize the surface of the earth.

Perhaps men will live more by night than by day. Astronomers will erect their observatories in quiet mountain ravines and on peaks, because the huge sea of coloured light may disturb the study of the heavens.

All this is not a modern concept – the great Gothic master-builders thought of it first. We must not forget that.

85 The brilliant (diamond) effect in architecture

Brilliants are treasured on the hands and neck, but in architecture the diamond effect is by no means prized. I suggest that this only happens because the brilliant is too small and architecture is too big. Large glass brilliants, however, can be produced of pumpkin size, without becoming too expensive. Will architecture despise the brilliant effect, when glass can be seen everywhere in large quantities? That seems to me unlikely. It is no argument against coloured glass that primitive people and small children are enraptured by it.

86 Three-dimensional and two-dimensional ornament in architecture

In the Alhambra, we mostly find three-dimensional ornament, but of perishable plaster-work. Glass architecture can also use such ornament, but of imperishable glass materials. The most delicate blown decoration is made of glass, even of frosted and filigree glass. This kind of plastic art for the ornamental glass wall should admittedly only be considered for formal rooms; there it is entirely feasible and not merely a figment of the imagination. Venice is no longer the pinnacle of glass culture, although it has contributed much that often obliges one to return to it later. I do not recommend copies, but it certainly seems to me that the splendours of Venetian glass, as reflected in particular by the palaces of Isola Bella, are valuable sources of inspiration. One often forgets that present-day Italy, without glass, really has very little attraction.

87 The transformation of fireworks

When there is more glass everywhere, fireworks will be transformed; thousands of reflection effects will be possible. But this chapter must wait until pyrotechnics have been further developed.

88 Colour-lit pools, fountains and waterfalls

This chapter shall be left to the landscape architects. They will tackle the job with great enthusiasm and be determined to offer more than the rococo period offered us.

89 The discovery of the brick bacillus

Brick decays. Hence fungus. The discovery of the brick bacillus is no great discovery, but now the doctor also has a major interest in finally ousting the cult of brick.

In the cellars of brick houses the air is always full of brick bacilli; glass architecture needs no cellars beneath it.

90 The nervous effect of very bright light unsoftened by colour

We have to thank very bright lights, in part, for the nervous ailments of our time. Light softened by colour calms the nerves. In many sanatoria it is recommended by nerve doctors as beneficial.

91 Railway stations and glass architecture

For station premises, which have to be screened at least partially against wind and rain, glass architecture is so appropriate that nothing further needs to be said about it.

92 Uniform street-lamps and their elimination

If we must mention something detestable, this is, in my view, those street lamps which in every town look so alike that one cannot help wondering how mankind can be capable of such monotonous repetition. Happily, this repetition can be quickly eliminated by combinations of coloured glass hanging-lamps, which are adaptable to a vast number of forms. This elimination will of course come very soon.

93 Present-day travel

Today people travel from nervous habit: they want to have something different, and although they know that all hotels and towns, mountain villages and health resorts have a dreadful sameness, they travel there just the same. They travel, knowing well that they will find nothing better wherever they go.

94 Future travel

In the future, people will travel in order to look at new glass architecture, which will differ widely in various parts of the world.

To travel for the sake of glass architecture has at all events a meaning; one may surely expect new glass effects in other places. One may also assume that nine-tenths of the daily press will report only on new glass effects. The daily press wants novelty – so it will not be unfriendly to glass.

95 The Doppler and the Zeeman effect

It has often been said that glass is not a 'precious' commodity.

In contrast to this, remember Frauenhofer's lines of the glass spectrum. In addition, Christian Doppler discovered that light, when it approaches or recedes, breaks up Frauenhofer's lines into infra-red and ultra-violet. By using photography it has been possible to measure this, and from these measurements we know precisely whether stars of weak luminosity are approaching us or receding, and at what speed. Without glass the Doppler effect would not be discernible; I should think that this speaks volumes for the importance of glass.

The Zeeman effect occurs through the action of a magnetic field and a flame; the spectrum then shows Frauenhofer's lines suddenly triplicated. From these 'triplets' one can determine the existence of magnetic fields, which are detectable in sun-storms and explain the constitution of sun-spots. I believe that the Zeeman effect also speaks volumes for the importance of glass.

Thus one can no longer be permitted to describe glass as of little value; whoever does that has no right to be considered an educated person.

96 Which spheres of interest are fostered or endangered by glass architecture

The livelihood of masons and carpenters – from what has been said above – is clearly threatened; also that of the whole timber industry, joiners, turners, etc. But the process will not be so rapid that it will be impossible to assimilate those affected into other trades; they will have plenty of time to transfer to the metal and glass industries. Very many new skills are required, and nothing stands in the way of the change.

Admittedly, many locksmiths say that a mason could never become a locksmith; the locksmith only says this because he fears competition.

But the spheres which will inevitably be stimulated by glass architecture are principally heavy industry, the chemical dye industry and the glass industry.

97 Heavy industry

The introduction of iron into house-building will, beyond question, bring so many new orders to heavy industry that it could continue to exist even if all cannon-making were stopped. Accordingly, heavy industry would be well advised not to take the ideas discussed in this book too lightly; they will bring it great pecuniary advantages. In any case, heavy industry should note that there will be many new potential clients because of glass architecture.

98 The chemical dye industry

The same thing applies to the colour industry. Glass architecture will consume vast quantities of colour.

99 The glass industry

It is undeniable that the glass industry has the lion's share in glass architecture. The present scale of the industry, however, is inadequate for the greater demand; it must expand in proportion. The financial success which will result from this is quite incalculable.

100 The influence of coloured glass on the plant world

Glass architecture will also exercise an influence on botanical gardens; entirely colourless, plain glass will be gradually abandoned. Coloured glass will only be used externally, where it does not absorb too much light. The plants will then be exposed experimentally to coloured light, and the experts may well have some surprises. The experiments should not be carried out in haste.

101 Art in bridge building

There have been times when the engineer has had the upper hand over the architect; not unnaturally, for the engineer was more needed.

Today the engineer no longer wants to stuff all the fees into his pocket; he gladly allows half to the architect. This will soon be apparent in bridge building, where there are high artistic ambitions. One could wish that these related to glass architecture.

102 The transformation of the Earth's surface

So many ideas constantly sound to us like a fairy-tale, when they are not really fantastic or utopian at all. Eighty years ago, the steam railway came, and undeniably transformed the face of the earth. From what has been said so far the earth's surface will once again be transformed, this time by glass architecture. If it comes, a metamorphosis will occur, but other factors must naturally be taken into consideration, which cannot be discussed here.

The present brick 'culture' of the city, which we all deplore, is due to the railway. Glass architecture will only come if the city as we know it goes. It is completely clear to all those who care about the future of our civilisation that this dissolution must take place. To labour the point is useless.

We all know what is meant by colour; it forms only a small part of the spectrum. But we want to have that part. Infra-red and ultra-violet are not perceptible to our eyes – but ultra-violet is perceptible to the sensory organs of ants. If we cannot at the moment accept that our sensory organs will develop appropriately overnight, we are justified in accepting that we should first reach for what is within our grasp – i.e., that part of the spectrum which we are able to take in with our own eyes – in fact, the miracles of colour, which we are in a position to appreciate ourselves. In this, only glass architecture, which will inevitably transform our whole lives and the environment in which we live, is going to help us. So we must hope that glass architecture will indeed transform the face of our world.

103 The transformation of the official architect

When the private client wants to build, he looks for the best architect. When the state wants to build, government architects are at its disposal – not the best architects, who are generally freelances. This is a deplorable situation, and it is the state that one chiefly deplores. These official architects, who are always hamstrung by bureaucracy (hence their inhibitions and conservatism), must once again become free; otherwise they will hinder future architectural progress. One sees from the buildings produced by official architects that they are scared of colour; scared of ridicule. This remarkable colour-shyness stems from old Peter Cornelius who would have nothing to do with colour.

In the botanical gardens at Dahlem there is as yet no orchid house. This is bound to be a glass palace. Its construction must be already assigned to government architects. I am curious to see the result. Heating by (ceramic) stoves has been proposed, for they are supposed to be better-suited to orchids than central heating; I do not know whether the construction of the stoves is being entrusted to a government master-potter.

104 The psychological effects of the glass architectural environment

The peculiar influence of coloured glass light was already known to the priests of ancient Babylon and Syria; they were the first to exploit the coloured glass hanging lamp in the temples, and the coloured glass ampulla was later introduced into churches throughout Byzantium and in Europe. From these were developed the stained glass windows of the Gothic period; it is not to be wondered at that these make an especially festive impression, but such an impression from coloured glass is inevitably inherent in glass architecture; its effect on the human psyche can accordingly only be good, for it corresponds to that created by the windows of Gothic cathedrals and by Babylonian glass ampullæ. Glass architecture makes homes into cathedrals, with the same effects.

105 A composed and settled nation, when glass architecture comes

When home life has reached the stage where even the wildest fancies appear to be realised, the longing for something different ceases; people will travel only to learn about a particular type of glass art and possibly to bring it home – to be able to reproduce it in a similar design.

Perhaps somewhere one may discover the art of making glass fibres like brocade, so that the fibres, viewed from different angles, will show different colour effects. Perhaps somewhere they can make a lace-like fabric from glass fibres and fix it to a darker glass wall of one colour; an intimate effect might result, and this would make for a homely atmosphere, which one would leave reluctantly; a curtain effect would be created. Perhaps then one would only travel to find out about new glass crafts; much that was new might emerge from old designs. But the entirely new is also to be expected from the great inventors of our own and future times.

106 More coloured light!

We must not strive to increase the intensity of light – today it is already too strong and no longer endurable. But a gentler light is worth striving for. Not more light! – 'more coloured light!' must be the watchword.

107 The main entrance

The pyramids are monumental. Cologne cathedral, too, is monumental – the Eiffel tower is also often so described nowadays, but the idea of what is monumental will be changed by glass architecture. Glass towers will be built deep in the sea, creating a special kind of luxury architecture, cool and very peaceful. Many people might think of giant windmills, with sails over a hundred metres long; but town hall and powder-magazine towers might not be suitable for windmill purposes; brick architecture would not stand up to a severe storm.

108 The monumental

In my opinion, the entrance to a great palace should always be an open hall of many glass walls, gathered together one upon another like the petals of an exquisite flower. The best architects should devote themselves particularly to entrance-hall construction, and then invite the interior designers to surpass the complicated architectonic effects. This should create a splendid challenge; and it would simply be necessary for the client to bear the cost and not come to the end of his financial resources too quickly.

109 Streets and highways as light-column avenues

The verges of streets and highways will no longer be planted with trees, which are not high enough for the purpose, but columns of light, provided with festoons of lights and shedding constantly changing coloured light, would be highly appropriate for verges.

110 Chemistry and technics in the twentieth century

We are not at the end of a cultural period – but at the beginning. We still have extraordinary marvels to expect from technics and chemistry, which should not be forgotten. This ought to give us constant encouragement. Unsplinterable glass should be mentioned here, in which a celluloid sheet is placed between two sheets of glass and joins them together.

111 Glass culture

After all the above, we can indeed speak of a glass culture. The new glass environment will completely transform mankind, and it remains only to wish that the new glass culture will not find too many opponents. It is to be hoped, in fact, that glass culture will have ever fewer opponents; to cling to the old is in many matters a good thing; in this way at any rate the old is preserved. We, too, want to cling to the old – the pyramids of ancient Egypt should most certainly not be abolished.

But we also want to strive after the new, with all the resources at our disposal; more power to them!

ALPINE ARCHITECTURE

by

Bruno Taut

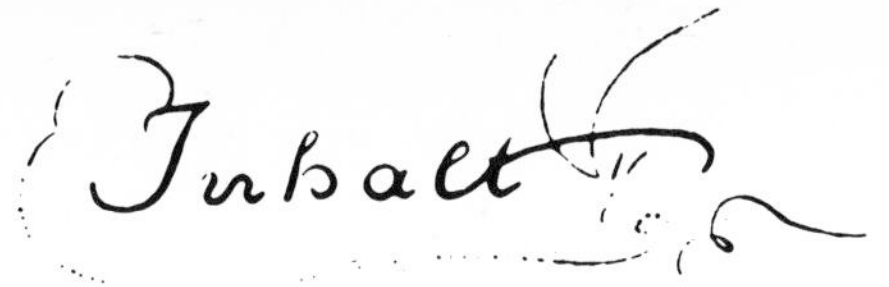

Niedergezeichnet Frühjahr u. Sommer

1917

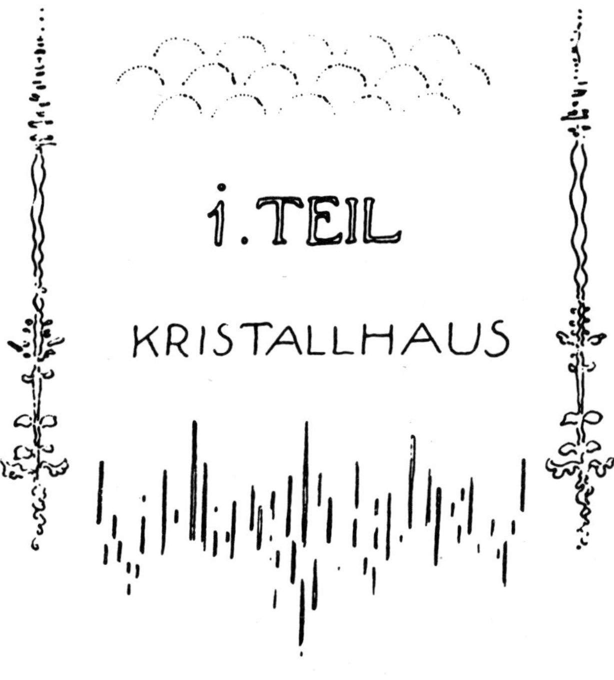

1 – 4

Turm am
Gebirgsee ~
an ihm Lan-
dungsstelle und
Treppenaufgang
(auf der abge-
wandten Seite)
Turmhelm aus
Kupfer, blank
vergoldet ~
Stangen blank
versilbert ~

Von Terr
am Tur
steile Trep
als Aufs
zum Kris
hause ~
Schwerer
stieg ~
Spitze Po
sadenstan
an ihm
blanke
~ farb

1.

Weg zum Kristallhause im Wildbachtal
Die Schlucht wird überspannt von Bögen aus schwerem farbigem Glas. Sie verengen sich in dem enger werden-den Tal über dem im-mer wilder stürzenden Bach und werden da immer glühender und tiefer in den Farben – bis die engste Talenge bis weit nach oben von einem Glasbogen-gitter in allen Farben geschlossen wird.
IN DIESES GITTER SIND HARMONISCH ABGESTIMMTE ÄOLSHARFEN EINGESETZT

Kristallhaus in den Bergen

ganz aus Glaskristall
errichtet – farbigem
in der Schnee und Gletscherregion
Andacht
Unaussprechliches
Schweigen

Tempel des Schweigens

Weg vom
Tal her
Kristallmaste
sind Wegbe-
gleiter.
Sie funkeln
in der Sonne
und besonders
die grössten,
die sich im
Lichte drehen –
Kristall-
Standarten

Plateaus für
Luftlandungen

bare Gegensätze. Architektur lässt sich nicht „anwenden". Auch nicht auf Ideale
soll verstummen, wo die höchste Baulust, wo die Kunst spricht – fern von Hütten

Dieses Kristallhaus soll keine „Krone" sein. Wer kann
Alle krönen wollen: ! — — Und keine „Stadtkrone". Bruno
ut durfte nicht das Höchste, das Leere über eine Stadt
een. Architektur und Stadtdunst bleiben unüberbrück-
ascbengedanke FLÄCHEN KANTEN WÖLBUNGEN RAUM.
n

Im Kristallhause
„Gesprochen darf in den Tempeln nicht werden, hineinkommen kann man immer - auch in der Nacht. Aber etwas, das unserem Gottesdienste entspräche giebt es hier nicht - sie wirken allein durch ihre erhabene Architektur und durch die grosse Stille, die nur von Zeit zu Zeit von feiner Orchester- und Orgelmusik unterbrochen wird. Ein paar grossartige kosmische Gemälde und Skulpturen sind zuweilen zu sehen - aber das Sichtbarzumachende wird immer seltener gezeigt, da es nicht in Einklang mit den überwältigenden Gefühlen der Weltverehrung zu bringen ist, wenn zu oft auf Einzelnes und Bestimmtes hingewiesen wird." (Scheerbart in Münchhausen und Clarissa)
Baumaterial ist nur Glas. Zwischen der Glashaut des Raumes und der äusseren Glashaut des Hauses ist ein grosser Zwischenraum zur Wärmung und zum Luftausgleich. Beide Häute entsprechen einander nicht. Das ist garnicht nötig. Auch am Körper erkennt man nicht von aussen die Eingeweide. Obere, Wände sind ausgebaucht, darunter Galerie für Musik und Zugang zum Turm und zu den Aussichtsbalkons. Alle Nützlichkeitsanlagen im Sockelgeschoss u. Unterbau der Terrassen: Unterkunft- und Erfrischungsräume, Fliegerschuppen, Heizung u.s.w. Das Nützliche soll nur funktionieren und möglichst wenig in die Erscheinung treten

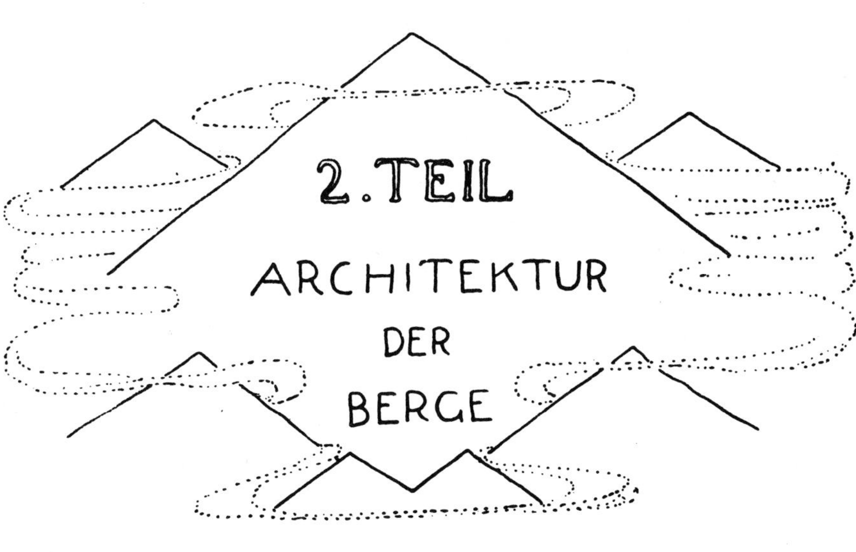

5 - ii

Pfeiler und Bögen von smaragdgrünem
Berges ragen aus dem Wolkenmeere
geöffneten Raumes. Architektur und

ßer der Schneekuppe eines hohen
Architektur des Gerüstes, des ins All
nicht untrennbare Begriffe

In der Tiefe
See mit
Schmuck aus
im Wasser.
Dieser und die
Wände leuchten
Nachts
Ebenso die
Bergspitzen.
Sie sind mit
glatten Kri-
stallspitzen
besetzt.
Scheinwerfer
auf den Bergen
lassen
diese Spitzen
in der Nacht
hell
auffunkeln

Der
ristallberg
Der Fels ist
oberhalb der
Vegetations-
zone behauen
und geglättet
zu vielfachen
kristallinischen
Formen.
Die hinteren
Schneekuppen
sind mit
Glasbögen-
architektur
bebaut
Vorne Kristall-
nadelpyra-
miden
Über dem Ab-
grund eine
Brückenver-
gitterung aus
Glas
7

GROTESKE
GEGEND
MIT
BEARBEITETEN
BERGSPITZEN

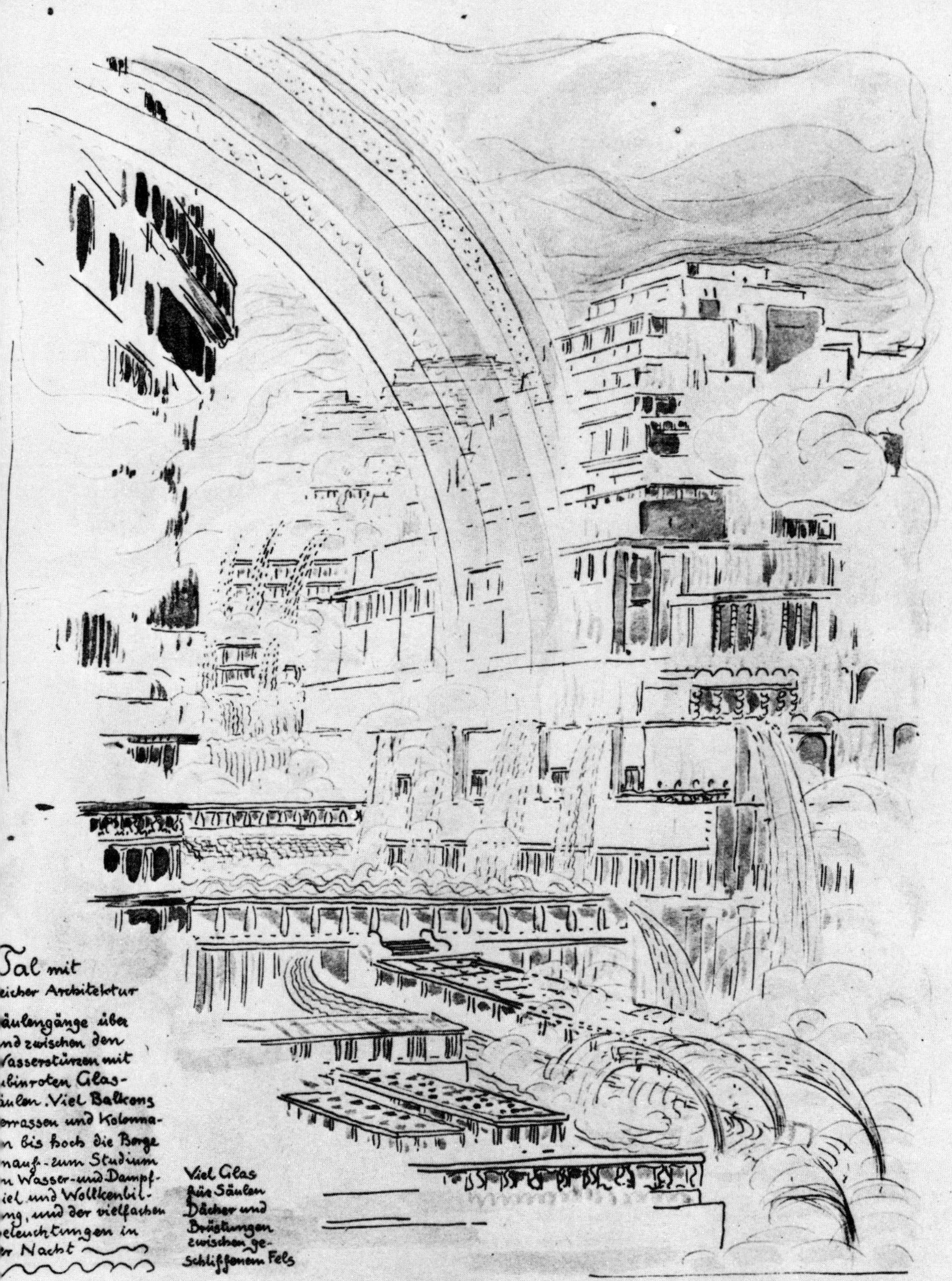
Tal mit
eicher Architektur
äulengänge über
nd zwischen den
Vasserstürzen mit
ubinroten Glas-
äulen. Viel Balkons
errassen und Kolonna-
n bis hoch die Berge
nauf - zum Studium
n Wasser- und Dampf-
iel und Wolkenbil-
ng, und der vielfachen
eleuchtungen in
r Nacht
Viel Glas
für Säulen
Dächer und
Brüstungen
zwischen ge-
schliffenem Fels

SCHNEE
GLETSCHER
GLAS
Firnen
im ewigen Eise
und Schnee ~
überbaut und ge-
schmückt mit
Umbauungen, Flä-
chen und Blöcken
von farbigem Glase
~ Bergblüten ~

Die Ausführung ist gewiss ungeheuer schwer und opfervoll, aber nicht unmöglich. „Man verlangt so sel
von den Menschen das Unmögliche" (Goethe)

In der Taltiefe
zwischen kristallisch-
kantig bearbeiteten
Bergen ^ ^ ^ ^ ^
Man sieht von oben
urch das Gewölbe
aus durchsichtigem
lase in den Raum
mit seinen gewölbe-
ragenden Säulen.
ie Seitenschiffe des
omes liegen in dem
usgehauenen Felsen
nd setzen sich in
Höhlen und
Grotten fort.
Im Bergineren
erglänzen die Kost-
barkeiten der künst-
lich beleuchteten
Glasarchitektur
Der Dom und seine Sei-
tenschiffe sind vom küh-
len Tageslicht erfüllt.
Nachts aber strahlt
er sein Licht auf die
Berge und zum Fir-
mament ^ ^ ^ Zweck
des Domes ? - Keiner -
wem nicht Andacht
in der Schönheit
genügt.
DER FELSEN DOM

3. TEIL

DER ALPENBAU

i2 - 2i

GROSS IST DIE NATUR
wig schön – eine ewige
Schöpferin, im Atom und im
Bergriesen. Alles ein ewiges
NEUSCHAFFEN.
Auch wir sind ihre Atome
und folgen ihrem Gebot –
im Schaffen.
Sie untätig anstaunen
ist sentimental.
SCHAFFEN
WIR
IN IHR UND
MIT IHR UND
SCHMÜCKEN
WIR
SIE!
2331 m
Der Vorderglärnisch bei
Glarus in der Schweiz.
Kahlgrauer Fels über
dem Vegetationsgrün.
Seine zufälligen Formen sollen kantig-
glatt werden, in
ihn eingelassen
weiss-gläserne
Kristalle, funkelnd in
der harten
Fassung
Auch in den
Tiefen der Wälder solche
Kristalle
Die Stadt Glarus
Piz Chalchagn 3154 m
Roseg-Tal
Roseg-Gletscher
Lanzettblattförmige Wände ragen aus den Wäldern auf.
In Betonfassung von weissem
Milchglas, in den Spitzen
und Einlagen rubinrot.
Diese erglühen des Nachts von innen erleuchtet. Die obersten Spitzen und die vor dem Gletscher zinnoberrot
Pontresina i. d. Schweiz

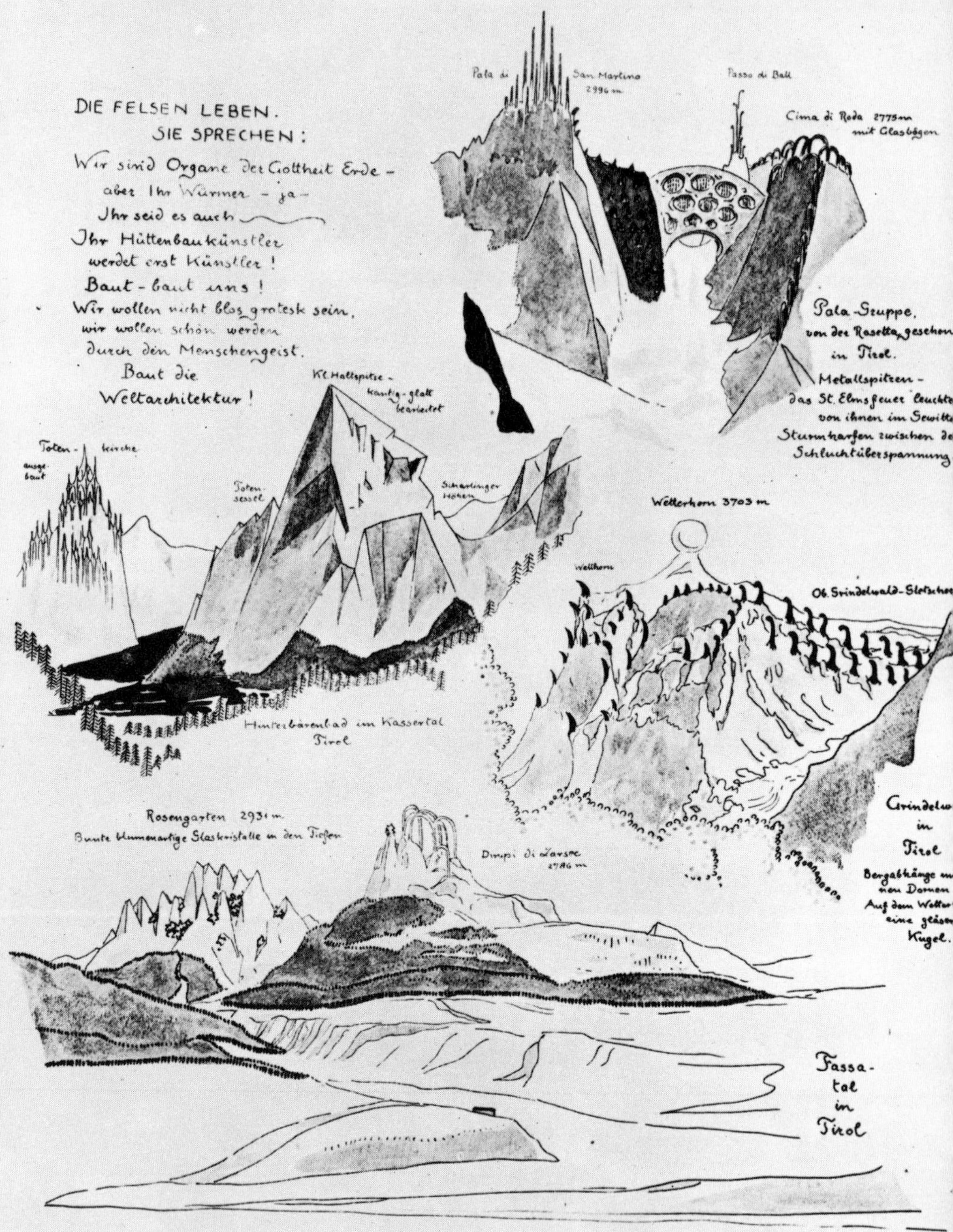

DIE FELSEN LEBEN.
SIE SPRECHEN:
Wir sind Organe der Gottheit Erde –
aber Ihr Würmer – ja –
Ihr seid es auch
Ihr Hüttenbaukünstler
werdet erst Künstler!
Baut – baut uns!
Wir wollen nicht bloß grotesk sein,
wir wollen schön werden
durch den Menschengeist.
Baut die
Weltarchitektur!
Pala di
San Martino
2996 m
Passo di Ball
Cima di Roda 2775 m
mit Glasbögen
Pala-Gruppe,
von der Rosetta gesehen
in Tirol.
Metallspitzen –
das St. Elmsfeuer leuchte
von ihnen im Gewitte
Sturmharfen zwischen de
Schluchtüberspannung
Kl. Hallspitze –
kantig-glatt
bearbeitet
Toten-
kirche
ausge-
baut
Toten-
sessel
Scharlinger
Höhen
Hinterbärenbad im Kaisertal
Tirol
Wetterhorn 3703 m
Wellhorn
Ob. Grindelwald-Gletscher
Grindelw
in
Tirol
Bergabhänge m
Domen
Auf dem Wetter
eine gläser
Kugel.
Rosengarten 2931 m
Bunte blumenartige Glaskristalle in den Tiefen
Dirupi di Larsec
2786 m
Fassa-
tal
in
Tirol

Der
Monte Resegone 1876 m bei Lecco
am Comersee
Aufbauten vorwiegend aus Glas
Tafelberg bei Garda
.. GLASKRISTALL
Der Monte San
Salvatore an
der Bucht von
~Lugano~
Ausgebaut durch
Felsanbauten und
-aussprengungen
um die „Naturform"
Terrassen für Flug-
landung und als
Zuschauerraum für Flug-,
Ballon-, Licht- und Wasser-
vorführungen.
Horizontkorrekturen

ALPENAUSLÄUFER AN DER RIVIERA ·

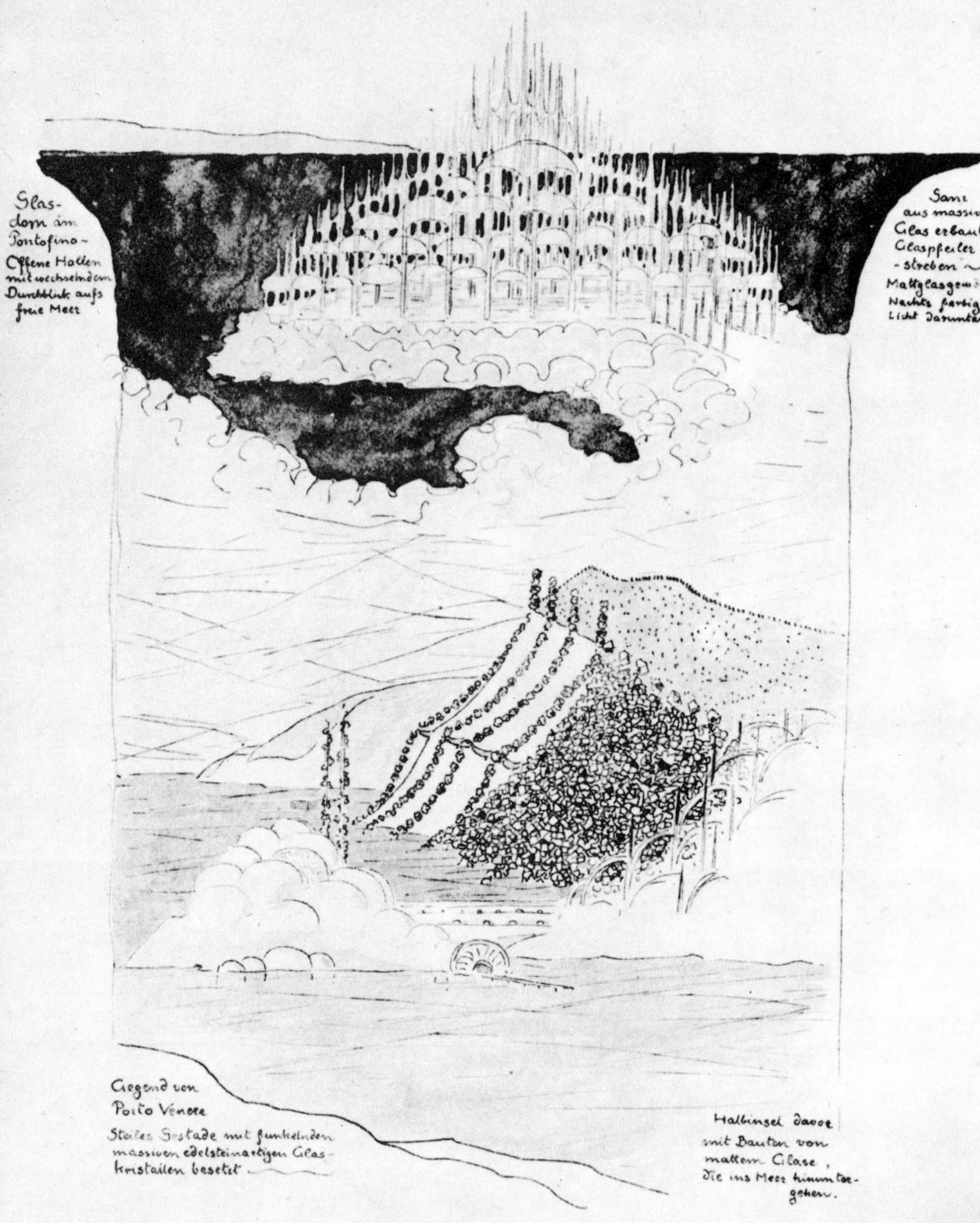

Glas-
dom am
Portofino –
Offene Hallen
mit wechselndem
Durchblick aufs
freie Meer
Ganz
aus massivem
Glas erbaut –
Glaspfeiler un
– streben –
Mattglasgewölbe
Nachts farbiges
Licht darunter –
Gegend von
Porto Venere
Steiles Gestade mit funkelnden
massiven edelsteinartigen Glas-
kristallen besetzt
Halbinsel davor
mit Bauten von
mattem Glase,
die ins Meer hinunter-
gehen.

VÖLKER EUROPAS!

BILDET EUCH DIE HEILIGEN GÜTER – BAUT! SEID EIN GEDANKE EURES STERNS, DER ERDE, DIE SICH SCHMÜCKEN WILL – DURCH EUCH!

Schematische Karte des Baugebiets

in fester Plan
werde begonnen,
egrenzt und –
escheiden: ~

No die höchste
lpenkette vom
Iontblanc her
n Monte Rosa
ber die italienische
ene herausragt,
n inneren Bogen
s Gebirgszuges –
a soll die Schön –
eit erstrahlen ~
er Monte Rosa
nd sein Vorgebirge
s zur grünen Ebene
ll umgebaut werden.

Ja, unpraktisch u. ohne Nutzen! Aber sind wir vom Nützlichen glücklich geworden? – Immer Nutzen und Nutzen: Comfort, Bequemlichkeit, – gutes Essen, Bildung – Messer, Gabel, Eisenbahnen, Closets und doch auch ~ ~ Kanonen, Bomben, Mordgeräte! ~ Blos Nützliches und Bequemes wollen ohne höhere Idee ist Langeweile. Langeweile

bringt Zank, Streit und Krieg: Lüge, Raub, Mord, Elend, millionen-millionenfach fliessendes Blut. ~ Predigt: seid friedfertig! predigt die soziale Idee: „Ihr seid alle Brüder, organisiert euch, ihr könnt alle gut leben, gut gebildet sein und Frieden haben!" – Eure Predigt verhallt, solange Aufgaben fehlen, Aufgaben, die die Kräfte bis zum Äussersten, aufs Blut anspannen. ~ Spannt die Massen in eine grosse Aufgabe ein, die sie alle erfüllt, vom Geringsten bis zum Ersten. Die ungeheure Opfer an Mut, Kraft und Blut und an Milliarden verlangt. Die aber sinnfällig deutlich für alle in der Vollendung ist. Jeder sieht im grossen Gemeinsamen deutlich das Werk seiner Hände: jeder baut – im wahren Sinne. Alle dienen der Idee, der Schönheit – als Gedanken der Erde, die sie trägt ~ Die Langeweile verschwindet und mit ihr der Zank, die Politik und das verruchte Gespenst Krieg ~ Riesige Aufgaben erwachsen der Industrie, und sie wird sich rasch darauf einstellen. Die Technik ist immer nur Dienerin – und nun soll sie nicht mehr gemeinen Instinkten dienen, den unsinnigen Ausgeburten der Langeweile, sondern dem Streben des wahrhaft tätigen Menschengeistes ~ Vom Frieden braucht niemand zu sprechen, wenn es nicht mehr Krieg giebt. ES GIEBT NUR NOCH RASTLOSES MUTIGES ARBEITEN IM DIENST DER SCHÖNHEIT, IM UNTERORDNEN UNTER DAS HÖHERE ~

DAS UGEBIET, VOM
GENEROSO GESEHEN
Bergbekrönungen, -bearbeitungen, Täler ausge…t – wie
im Vorigen. Die Hochfläche am Lugano-See
mit gestaffelter, von oben mosaikartig wirkender
Glasarchitektur bebaut.

Flugzeuge und Luftschiffe fahren Glückliche, die froh sind, von Krankheit und Leid durch Anschauen ihres Werkes befreit zu sein – in seligen Augenblicken. Reisen! und auf der Reise das Werk entstehen und erfüllt zu sehen, an dem man als Arbeiter irgendwie im fernen Lande mitgewirkt hat! Unsere Erde, bisher eine schlechte Wohnung, werde eine gute Wohnung

MONTE ROSA LYSKAMM BREITHORN MATTERHORN

DIE SCHNEE- UND EISKETTE DES MONTE ROSA VOM GORNERGRAT

Die Kosten sind ungeheure, und welche Opfer! – Aber nicht für Machtsucht, Mord und Elend

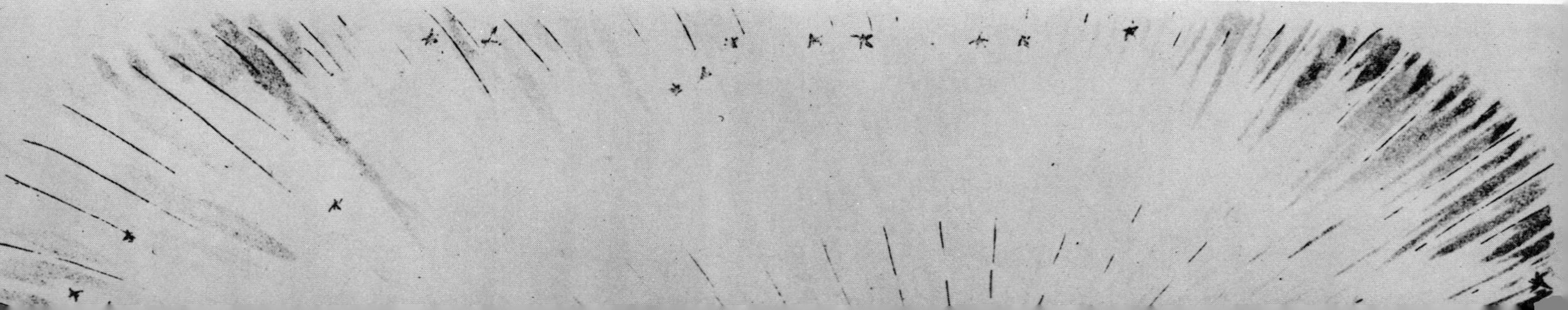

MONTE ROSA BEBAUUNG – Glasglocke im gläsernen Streben Bögen und Kristallen

DER FELS MATTERHORN < < <

DIE BERGNACHT'

SCHEINWERFER UND LEUCHTENDE BAUTEN

SCHLUSS
DES 3. TEILS!

Aber das Höhere wissen! Das gewaltigste W
ist nichts ohne das Höhere. Wir müssen immer
Unerreichbare kennen und wollen, wenn das Erre
bare gelingen soll. Nur Gäste sind wir auf diese
Erde, und eine Heimat haben wir nur im H
heren, im Aufgehen darin und im Unterord

22 - 25

Die Ratak- und Ralik-Inselgruppen der Südsee

Die Andenkette ein leuchtendes Band von Kratern, Bergdomen u. Talbauten
Saum des grossen Meeres

LIEBE IST PHANTASIE

LIEBE ZUR ERDE — IHR BILD IN UNS

RÜGEN

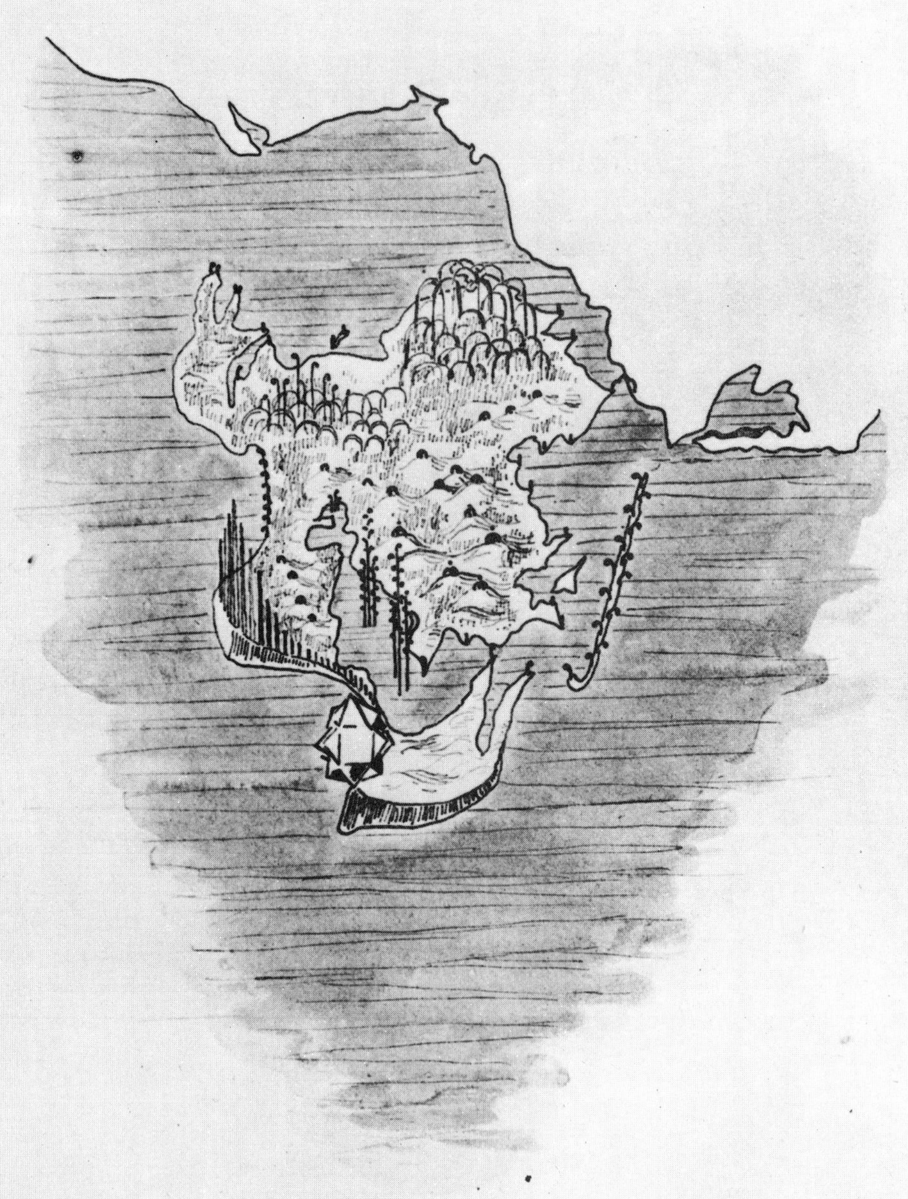

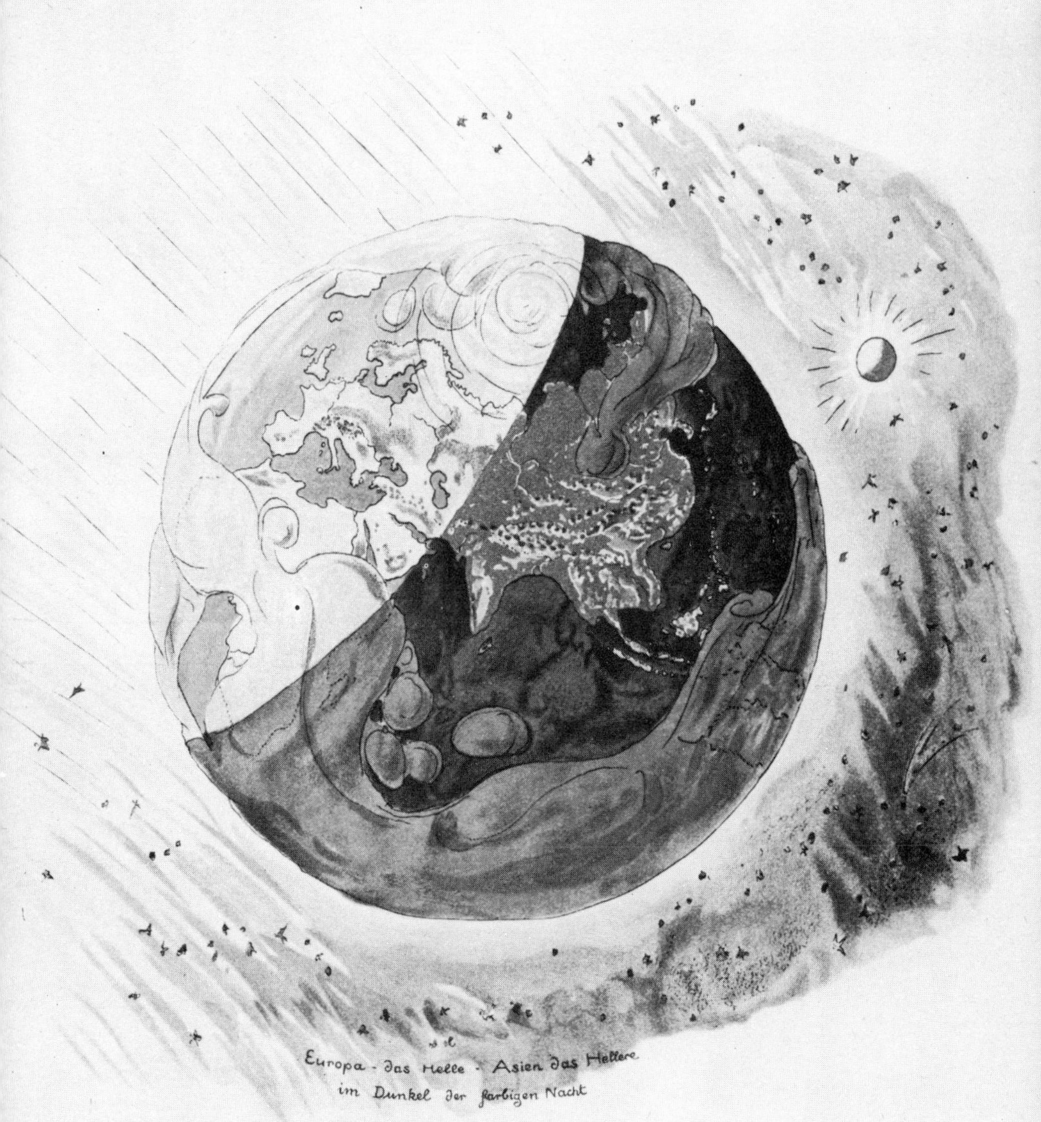

Europa - das Helle - Asien das Hellere
im Dunkel der farbigen Nacht

5. TEIL

STERNBAU

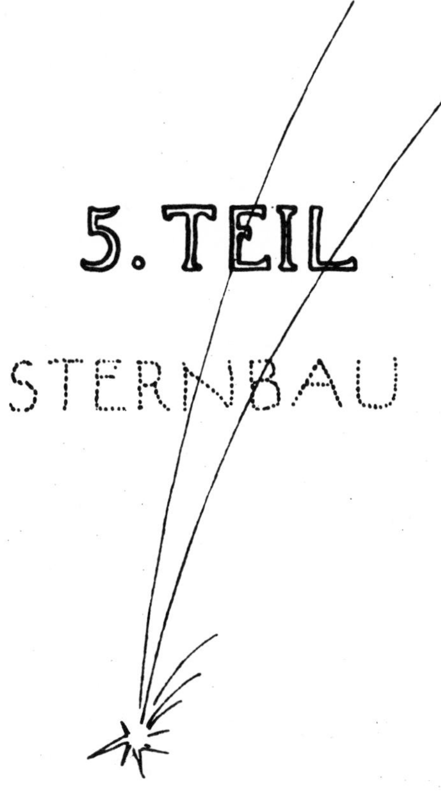

26 - 30

DOMSTERN

GROTTENSTERN
mit schwebender Architektur

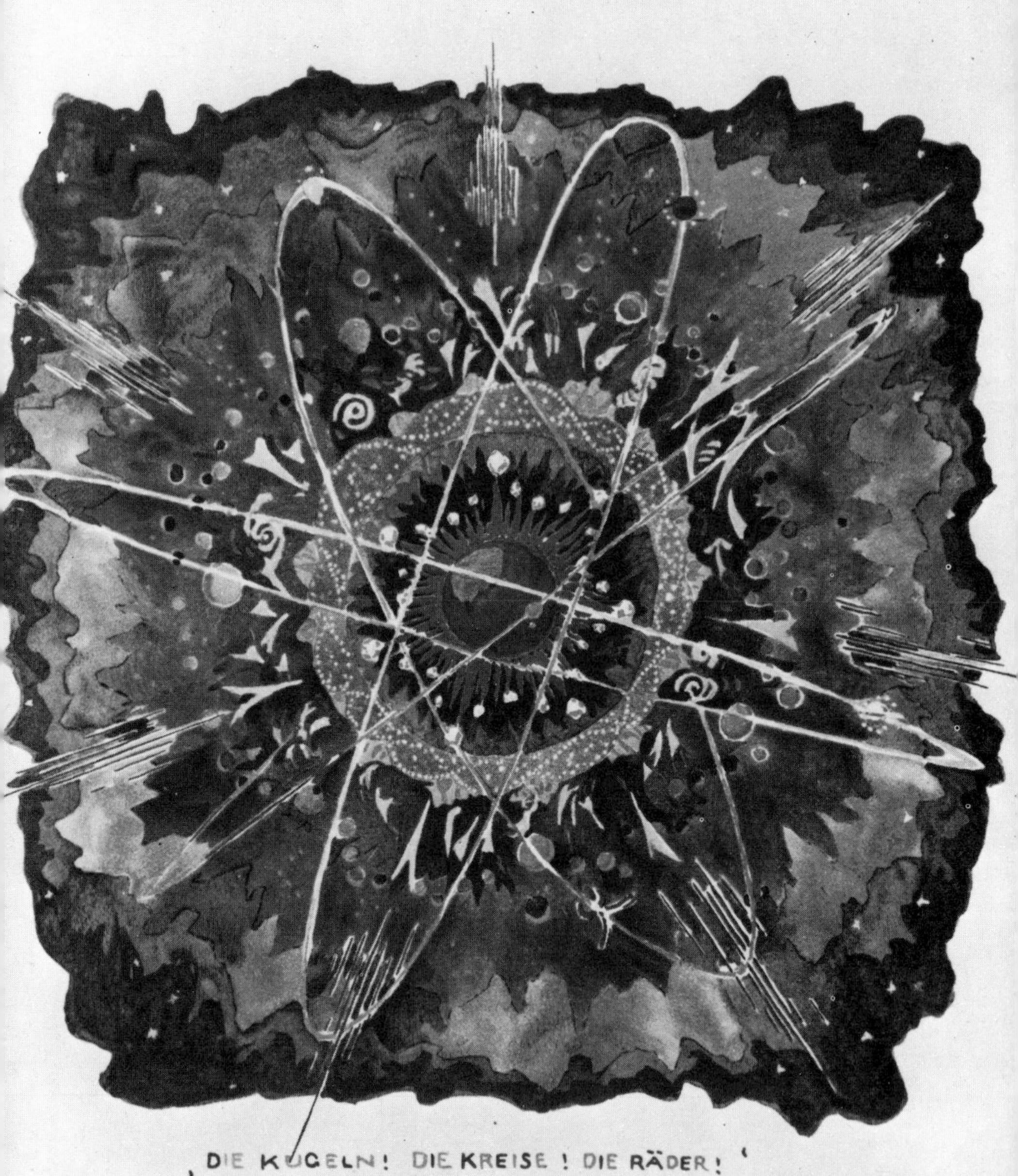

„DIE KUGELN! DIE KREISE! DIE RÄDER!“

Systeme von Systemen – Welten-Nebel

Sterne

Welten

Schlaf

Tod

DAS GROSSE

NICHTS

DAS

NAMENLOSE

Ende

English captions to Alpine Architecture

The numerals refer to the plate numbers

Part 1

THE CRYSTAL HOUSE

1

ASCENT TO THE CRYSTAL HOUSE

Tower beside a mountain lake – complete with landing stage and flight of steps (on the far side). Cupola of copper, brightly gilded. Shaft plated in gleaming silver.

Flights of steep steps lead up to the crystal house from the terrace by the tower – a difficult ascent. Beside the steps a palisade of pointed stakes, brightly coloured and gleaming.

2

PATH TO THE CRYSTAL HOUSE IN THE WILDBACHTAL

The gorge is spanned by arches of heavy coloured glass. They become progressively narrower as the valley closes in round the ever more turbulent torrent, becoming at the same time more glowing and of deeper colours. Until at its narrowest point the valley is closed by a lattice of glass arches of every hue.

IN THIS LATTICE ARE SET HARMONIOUSLY TUNED AEOLIAN HARPS.

3

CRYSTAL HOUSE IN THE MOUNTAINS

Built entirely of crystal glass – coloured. In the region of snowfields and glaciers. Prayer, inexpressible Silence. The Temple of Silence. The path up from the valley. Crystal masts border the way. They sparkle in the sun: particularly the tallest of them, which revolve in the light. Crystal standards. Landing pads for aerial landings.

This Crystal House is not intended to be a 'crown'! And certainly not a 'City's Crown'. Bruno Taut has no right to place the Most Sublime, the Void above a city. Architecture and the vapour of cities remain irreconcilable antitheses.

Architecture does not allow itself to be 'used'. Not even for Ideals. Every human thought must become silent when Art and Delight in Building speak – far away from foundries and barracks.

4

INSIDE THE CRYSTAL HOUSE

'No-one may speak in the Temples, entry is always possible – even in the night. But there is nothing here which corresponds to our church services – the Temples achieve their effect solely through their noble architecture, and through their great Silence, which is broken only from time to time by beautiful orchestral and organ music. A few Magnificent Cosmic paintings and sculptures can occasionally be seen – but these manifestations are shown at increasingly long intervals, since too frequent concentration upon the Singular and Particular is not in tune with the overpowering feelings of reverence for the world.' (Scheerbart in *Münchhausen und Clarissa.*)

Building material is of Glass only. Between the glass shell of the interior and the outer glass shell of the house is a large space, which serves for heating and ventilation. It is not in the least necessary for the two shells to correspond with each other, just as with the body one is not able to recognise the inner organs from the outside. The upper walls are hollowed out to form a music gallery and to give access to the tower and the observation balconies. All utilities are in the basement and in the foundations of the terraces: accommodation and refreshment rooms, aircraft hangars, heating etc.

The utilitarian is only required to function, and to show as little as possible.

Part 2

ARCHITECTURE IN THE MOUNTAINS

5

Pillars and arches of emerald green glass above the snow capped summit of a high mountain tower above the sea of clouds. The architecture of Framework of Space open to the Universe. Architecture and the House are not inseparable ideas.

6

VALLEY TRANSFORMED INTO A FLOWER

In the Depth of a lake with flower-like decorations made of glass in the water. Together with the walls they glow at night. Likewise the peaks of the mountains. They are set with smooth crystal mushrooms. Searchlights on the mountains pick out the bright twinkling of the peaks at night.

Walls of coloured glass in rigid frames are set up on the slopes. The beams of light bring out many changing effects, both for those who walk in the valleys and between the valleys – and for those who see them from the air. The aerial view will bring great changes to Architecture – and to Architects.

7

THE CRYSTAL MOUNTAIN

The rock above the treeline is hewn away and smoothed into many-faceted crystalline forms.

The snow-domes in the background are covered with an architecture of glass arches. In the foreground, pyramids of crystal shafts. Above the chasm, a bridge-like trellis of glass.

8

GROTESQUE REGION with ELABORATELY DECORATED MOUNTAIN PEAKS

9

VALLEY RICHLY DECORATED WITH ARCHITECTURE

Arcades above and between the waterfalls with pillars of ruby-red glass. Many balconies, terraces and colonnades reaching high up into the mountains – for the study of the play of water and steam and the formation of clouds and for multiple illuminations at night.

Much glass for pillars, roofs and balustrades between smooth-cut rock.

10

SNOW, GLACIER, GLASS

SNOWFIELDS in regions of eternal ice and snow – built over and decked with embellishments in the form of planes and blocks of coloured glass. Mountain flowers.

The execution would most certainly involve unheard of difficulties and sacrifices, but would not be impossible. 'The Impossible is so seldom required of Man' (Goethe).

11

THE ROCK-CATHEDRAL

In the depths of the valley, between mountains hewn into crystalline angles . . . From above, one can see through the vaulting of transparent glass into the interior with its pillars supporting the vault. The aisles of the Cathedral are situated in the hollowed-out rock, and continue in caves and grottoes.

In the bowels of the mountain the jewel-like glass architecture shimmers in the artificial light. The Cathedral and its side aisles are filled with cool daylight. At night, however, its light shines forth into the Mountains and the Heavens . . . The purpose of the Cathedral? None – if prayer in the midst of beauty is not sufficient.

Part 3

ALPINE BUILDING

12

NATURE IS GREAT!

Ever beautiful – eternally creating, in miniature and on the largest scale. Everything is eternally being RE-CREATED. We, also, are her miniatures and follow her behest – in creating. It is sentimental to stand idly admiring. LET US CREATE IN HER AND WITH HER AND LET US DECORATE HER!

Vorderglärnisch near Glarus in Switzerland. Bare grey rock, rising from the green of the forests. Its haphazard shape must be smoothed into angular planes. Crystalline shapes of white glass shimmer in their rocky setting. More such crystals in the depth of the forests.

The town of Glarus; Piz Chalchagn 3154 m; Roseg Valley; Roseg Glacier; Pontresina in Switzerland.

Lancet-shaped panels rise up out of the woods. Of white opalescent glass in concrete frames, the points and inlays ruby-red. They glow at night with inner lighting. The topmost points and those of the glacier picked out in vermilion.

13

THE ROCKS LIVE. THEY SPEAK: We are the voice of the Deity Earth – but you worms – yes – you are also her voice. You artists of factory building become real artists for the first time! Build – build us! We have no wish to be merely grotesque, we want to be beautiful through the Spirit of Man.

Build the architecture of the World!

Totenkirche embellished. Totensessel. Kl. Haltspitze, hewn into smooth angular planes. Scharlinger Höhen. Hinterbärenbad in the Kassertal, Tyrol. Passo di Ball. Pala di San Martino 2996 m. Cima di Roda 2775 m with glass arches. The Pala Group seen from Rosetta in the Tyrol. Metal points – St Elmo's Fire gleams from them during thunderstorms. A harp that sounds in a storm in the bridge over the chasm. Wetterhorn 3703 m. Wellhorn. Upper Grindelwald Glacier. Grindelwald in the Tyrol. Mountain walls studded with iron thorns. A glass sphere on the summit of the Wetterhorn.

Rosengarten 2931 m. Bright flower-like glass crystals in the hollows. Dirupi di Larsec 2786 m. Fassatal in the Tyrol.

14

Monte Resegone 1876 m., near Lecco on the Lake of Como.

Superstructures mainly of Glass.

Table mountain near Garda . . . crystal glass.

Monte San Salvatore in the Bay of Lugano. Transformed by additions of rock – and by blasting – into the shape of 'natural' terraces for aerial landings and as a grandstand for displays by aircraft, balloons, light and water.

15

ALPINE SPURS REACHING TO THE RIVIERA

Glass dome in Portofino – Open halls with changing views of the open sea.

Built completely out of solid glass – glass columns and buttresses – dim glass vaulting illuminated at night with coloured light.

Area around Porto Venere. Steeply sloping shore set with solid, jewel-like crystals of glass.

Peninsula in front of it with buildings of opaque glass going down to the sea.

16

PEOPLE OF EUROPE! FASHION FOR YOURSELVES A HOLY ARTEFACT – BUILD! REFLECT THE DESIRES OF YOUR STAR, THE EARTH WHO WOULD DECK HERSELF – THROUGH YOU!

Schematic map of the building area

Let work begin on a firm plan, limited and – modest: let beauty shine forth from the area where the highest mountain range extends from Mont Blanc to Monte Rosa, towering over the North Italian Plain, in the inner curve of the mountain range. Monte Rosa and its attendant peaks, must be transformed right down to the green plain.

Yes! impracticable and without profit! But has the useful ever made us happy? – Profit and even more profit: Comfort, Convenience – Good Living, Education – knife and fork, railways and water-closets: and then – guns, bombs, instruments for killing! – Merely to desire the useful and the comfortable without higher ideas spells boredom. Boredom brings quarrelling, strife and war: lies, robbery, murder and wretchedness, blood flowing from a million wounds. Preach: be peaceable! Preach: the social Concept: the Brotherhood of Man. Get organised! and you can all live well, all be well educated and at peace! – – As long as there are no tasks to be done your preaching will echo emptily – – Tasks that demand the last ounce of effort, the last drop of blood – – Harness the masses – for a gigantic task, in the completion of which each man will feel himself fulfilled, to be the humblest or the most exalted. A task whose completion can be felt to have meaning for all. Each man will see his own handiwork clearly in the common achievement: each man will build – in the true sense. All men will serve the one concept, Beauty – as the image of the Earth that bears them. – – Boredom disappears, and with it strife, politics and the evil spectre of War. – – – Gigantic tasks stimulate Industry, which quickly gears itself up for them. Engineering is merely a servant – and it will now no longer be called upon to serve base instincts, and the senseless by-products of boredom, but to serve the positive strivings of the human spirit. – – – There will be no more need to speak of Peace when there is no more War.

THERE WILL ONLY BE CEASELESS AND COURAGEOUS WORK IN THE SERVICE OF BEAUTY, IN SUBORDINATION TO HIGHER THINGS.

17

THE BUILDING REGION SEEN FROM MONTE GENEROSO

Crowns on the mountains – decorations, valleys transformed as in the foregoing. The plateau round the Lake of Lugano built over with graduated glass architecture, which gives the effect of mosaic when seen from above.

Aircraft and airships transport their passengers on pleasure trips to find joy and release from sickness and sorrow through the contemplation of their own handiwork. To travel! And on the journey to see the growth and completion of the work to which one has in some measure contributed as a worker in a far-off country! Let our Earth, till now a poor habitation, become a pleasant place to live in.

18

THE SNOW AND ICE RANGE OF MONTE ROSA SEEN FROM THE GORNERGRAT

The cost would be colossal, and what sacrifices would have to be made! But not out of a craving for power, murder and wretchedness.

19

THE EMBELLISHMENT OF MONTE ROSA – Glass bell with glass buttresses, arches and crystals.

20

THE ROCK of the MATTERHORN – – – –

21

NIGHT IN THE MOUNTAINS. SEARCHLIGHTS AND ILLUMINATED BUILDINGS.

But higher knowledge! The greatest work is nothing without the Sublime. We must always recognise and strive for the unattainable if we are to achieve the attainable. We are but guests upon this earth, and our true home is only in the Sublime: in merging with it and in subordinating ourselves to it.

Part 4

TERRESTRIAL BUILDING

22

The Ratak and Ralik Archipelago in the South Sea.

23

The mountain range of the Andes a gleaming band of craters, mountain domes and peopled valleys bordering the Pacific.

LOVE IS IMAGINATION
Love of the Earth – Her image is in us.

24

RUGEN

25

Europe – the bright one – Asia still brighter in the coloured darkness of the night.

Part 5

ASTRAL BUILDING

26

THE CATHEDRAL STAR

27

CAVERN-STAR with suspended architecture.

28

'GLOBES! CIRCLES! WHEELS!'

29

Systems within systems – Worlds – Nebulæ.

30

Stars. Worlds. Sleep. Death. Immensity. Nothingness. Namelessness. The End.